Ghosts of Hershey and Vicinity

Christopher E. Wolf

Schiffer Publishing Ltd

4880 Lower Valley Road, Atglen, Pennsylvania 19310

Dedication

I'd like to first and foremost dedicate this book to my lovely wife, Cindy, who alternatively cheered me on when I needed it and kicked me in the butt when necessary to keep this project on schedule.

Molten Choco © Rick Sargeant Bram Janssens. Photo courtesy of bigstockphotos.com.
Designed by "Sue"
Type set in A Charming Font Expanded/New Baskerville BT

ISBN: 978-0-7643-3285-2
Printed in The United States of America

Schiffer Books are available at special discounts for bulk purchases for sales promotions or premiums. Special editions, including personalized covers, corporate imprints, and excerpts can be created in large quantities for special needs. For more information contact the publisher:

Published by Schiffer Publishing Ltd.
4880 Lower Valley Road
Atglen, PA 19310
Phone: (610) 593-1777; Fax: (610) 593-2002
E-mail: Info@schifferbooks.com

For the largest selection of fine reference books on this and related subjects, please visit our web site at **www.schifferbooks.com**
We are always looking for people to write books on new and related subjects. If you have an idea for a book please contact us at the above address.

This book may be purchased from the publisher. Include $5.00 for shipping.
Please try your bookstore first. You may write for a free catalog.

In Europe, Schiffer books are distributed by
Bushwood Books
6 Marksbury Ave.
Kew Gardens
Surrey TW9 4JF England
Phone: 44 (0) 20 8392-8585; Fax: 44 (0) 20 8392-9876
E-mail: info@bushwoodbooks.co.uk
Website: www.bushwoodbooks.co.uk

Contents

Authors Note 4

Introduction 7

Chapter 1: Milton S. Hershey 11
    A Brief Look at the History of the Town of Hershey and
        the Man Who Created It 11

Chapter 2: The Hershey Theater 19

Chapter 3: Ghosts of the Park 29
    The Ghost Children of the Hershey Swimming Pool 35
    The Moaning Woman 36

Chapter 4: The Hershey Hotel 39

Chapter 5: The Ghosts of Cloverdale 49

Chapter 6: What if Mr. And Mrs. Hershey had Died
    on the Titanic? 55

Chapter 7: Eerie Ephrata 59
    Ghosts of the Revolutionary War in Ephrata? 60
    The Haunted Mountain Springs Hotel 62
    The Ghostly Twin of the Old Lincoln Farmhouse 67
    The Ghostly Swimmer 73
    The Ghost of Apple Street 77
    Is That You Poppi? 78

Chapter 8: Lebanon County Ghosts 89
    Inn 422 89
    The Rexmont Inn 96
    Moonshine Church 100
    The Headless Copter Pilot 104
    The Haunted Hunter 105

The Railroad Ghosts of Rausch Gap 108
The Kleinfeltersville Hotel 110
Haunts of Higher Learning 111
The Haunted Batdorf Building 112
Chapter 9: Haunts Nearby Hershey 115
Indian Echo Caverns 115
The Story of William Wilson and His Sister Elizabeth 117
Emma is Here! The Haunts of Alfred's
Victorian Restaurant 124
Chapter 10: Hauntings North of Hershey 127
The Red-Eyed Ghost 127
The Haunted Amity Hall Hotel 131
The Ghosts of the Greenhouse Mansion 134
The White Dogs and the Hanging Tree 139
West Perry High School's Ghostly Janitor 140
Chapter 11: Dauphin County Ghosts 141
Ghosts of the I.H.S. Nursing Home 141
The Haunted Mall 142
The Linglestown Vortex and the Ghost Children
of Gravity Hill 143
The Ghosts of Stony Valley 143
The Wolf Pond Monster 145
The Seven Elizabeths Cemetery 145
Chapter 12: A Word About Ghost Hunting 147
Appendix 153
The Pennsylvania Hex Files 153
Bibliography 157
Places Index 159

Author Note

All views expressed are by individuals and are not meant to be associated officially with any Hershey Industry. This book is not sponsored, endorsed, or otherwise affiliated with any Hershey Companies whose locations are listed herein. They include The Hotel Hershey, the Hershey Theater, Hersheypark, and The Milton S. Hershey School among others. This book is derived from the author's independent research.

Acknowledgments

A book doesn't get written in a vacuum. It requires a great number of helpful people to give birth to a brand-spanking new book. I'd like to thank everyone involved with making this project happen.

I'd like to thank Dinah Roseberry, my editor at Schiffer Books, for giving me the chance to be published.

A debt of gratitude goes to the staff of The Hotel Hershey: Kathy in the gift shop, Al Rossi, who pointed me to the "Misfits," Gloria and Llenay, whose stories of the hotel are a great boon to this book. A word of thanks to Amanda Knoll at the Book Cellar; her story was one of the first I acquired for this book and it helped lead to many other ones.

Many thanks to Elvira and Dale Ebling of the Derry-Hershey Historical Society for directing me to Al Rossi. A special thanks to my nephew, Douglas, who, like a good scout, is always prepared and helped out my investigation in the Hotel Hershey.

A round of thanks goes to Millie Morsis and the staff at the Hershey Theater. A heartfelt thanks to the folks at Inn 422, and last but not least, a very big thank you to my wife, Cindy, who not only kept this book project going, but also contributed some of the photos within its pages.

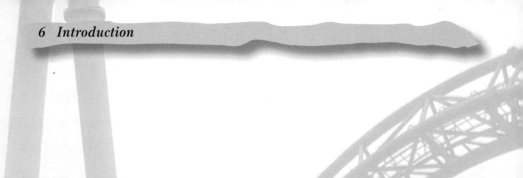

Downtown Hershey, Pennsylania. *Courtesy of Cindy Wolf*

(Inset) Downtown Hershey, Pennsylvania. Notice the twin smokestacks from the chocolate factory. *Courtesy of Cindy Wolf*

Introduction

Hershey... The sweetest, or most haunted, place on earth?

When most people think of Hershey's name, it either conjures up the image of the great American chocolate bar or the world-class amusement theme park located in Central Pennsylvania.

This book is an attempt at conjuring up a third option: ghosts and legends of Hershey. Why write a book of ghost stories about Hershey and the surrounding area? Simple. I collect and research ghost story books from places my wife and I have visited over the years, like people collecting souvenir t-shirts. In Hershey, it wasn't quite that easy. Last winter, we visited Hershey and I couldn't find a single book on ghost stories and legends for the Hershey area, so I decided to write one.

When you discuss the subject of ghosts and hauntings people generally fall into two categories: believers and nonbelievers. Believers are usually people who have had a paranormal experience of some type in their lives or are just naturally open minded. Nonbelievers, are usually show-me types of people who may be entertained by the notion of a ghost story, but don't really believe in them. All it usually takes, is one good personal encounter with the unexplained, no matter how small, to turn the nonbeliever into a believer. Whether you are of the first or second type of person is no difference. The ghost stories and legends that have been collected in this book are not here to prove the existence of ghosts. That's for you to decide. They are here for your enjoyment.

What Is a Ghost?

But just what is a ghost? Ghosts fall into different paranormal categories. There are several different types of ghosts. A common type of a ghost is found in somthing called a "Residual Haunting." A residual haunting is when a spirit keeps repeating the same action over and over again without interacting with the people who are witnessing the paranormal event. A spectral roller coaster that appears on the same date every year would be an example of a residual haunting.

Another type of haunting is one called an "Interactive Haunting." In this case, the ghost knows that it's a spirit and will possibly interact with the living. The ghost of Ann Coleman at the Inn 422 would fall under this category.

A "Poltergeist" is a special kind of spirit entity. Some paranormal researchers believe that the unconscious emotional energy that has been suppressed by either a pre-teen or teenager manifests itself subconsciously by affecting the surrounding area in which they are in. An example of poltergeist activity might be the Cloverdale ghost at the Milton Hershey school.

Many times a location is haunted because there is a long history associated with it or because a great trauma occurred there. Gettysburg, would be a prime example of a great battle causing many hauntings due to the massive amount of emotional energy and deaths that occurred there in a short period of time.

I personally believe the spirits that haunt the town of Hershey are there for a totally different emotional reason. Milton and Kitty Hershey put their hearts and souls into the founding of the town, and the reason their spirits chose to linger there is that they love the town and care about its future so much that they don't ever want to leave.

Many of the sightings of the spirit of Milton S. Hershey occurred during the 1970s when the largest renovation project in the history of the town took place. What's a more appropriate time for Milton Hershey to pay attention to what was going on in the town that he built from nothing? From ghostly crossdressing bankers, ghostly swimmers, and the lingering spirit of Milton Hershey, who just can't leave the place he loved so much while he was alive, they are all here.

The town of Hershey is active with countless ghosts, many of whom their stories are being told for the first time in the pages of this book. So the next time you're in Hershey, and enjoying one of the many tourist attractions, say a little thank you to Milton. You never know, he might just hear you and say, "You're welcome."

Chapter 1
Milton S. Hershey

*A Brief Look at the History of the Town of Hershey
and the Man Who Created It*

Hershey...What's the first thing you think of when you hear that name? Most people associate it with chocolate, but who was the man behind the chocolate confection that bears his name?

The birthplace of Milton S. Hershey.

Milton Snavely Hershey was born to Mennonite parents named Henry and Fannie Hershey on September 13, 1857, on a small farm near the community of Derry in central Pennsylvania. Born almost on the eve of the civil war, Milton Hershey lived through several amazing decades that formed the type of man who would accomplish many astonishing things in his life.

From an early age, his mother, Fannie, raised him in the strict Mennonite faith. His father, Henry, wasn't nearly so strict. Henry Hershey was a visionary, an entrepreneur, but not a very successful one. He was more of a ne'er do well and because he spent most of his time on get-rich-quick schemes, the Hersheys moved frequently—which in turn had an adverse effect on young Milton's education. Milton Hershey only attended school until the fourth grade. Even though most people nowadays would not consider that an education at all, Milton had enough education to start with and learned what ever else he needed on his own.

Perhaps it was the combination of the two different parenting styles that gave Milton the flexibility to become a huge success later in his life. On the one hand, he was greatly influenced by his Mother's common sense, strict self-discipline, and hard work in order to achieve a goal in life. On the other hand, Milton had inherited an open mind and the ability to think *outside the box* by his free-spirited father, Henry.

At the age of sixteen, young Milton started apprenticing with a candy maker in Lancaster City by the name of Royer. This was where he shined. He realized his life's passion was making confections.

After apprenticing four years at Royers, Milton was ready to strike out on his own. His mother was skeptical and thought that candy making was a frivolous vocation, yet she backed her son's dream to open a candy shop in Philadelphia. His aunt helped finance the venture, but as hard as Milton tried to make it a success, he failed after the first year in business.

Not one to be easily discouraged, Milton Hershey opened not just one, but two new shops. One shop was located in New York City and the other in Chicago. Unfortunately, both of these ventures failed as well.

In 1883, Hershey returned to Lancaster City and opened another factory called the Lancaster Caramel Company on Church Street. This was his first real successful company due in part to the way he'd learned to use fresh milk to make the caramel his company produced taste better and last on store shelves longer than his competitors' brand.

When he visited the 1893 World's Columbian Exposition in Chicago, Milton witnessed a demonstration of a German chocolate-making machine and became so excited that he bought the equipment on the spot and had it shipped directly to his Lancaster factory where he immediately began experimenting in mass producing chocolate.

Hershey still hadn't given up on making caramels, but seven years later, Milton decided to pursue chocolate making full-time. Taking a huge risk, he sold the Lancaster Caramel Company for the hefty sum of $1 million in 1900, just so he could focus all his attention on his new favorite business: Chocolate!

After searching for a new location to build his chocolate factory, he settled on the area of his birth, Derry Township.

As a side note, Hershey originally wanted to build his new factory outside of Lancaster City, but greedy city officials wanted to tax him more than other businesses were being taxed and he chose a more reasonably-taxed location. In all, it took him three years to find the perfect site, but Derry township had everything he needed, including farms with large fresh supplies of milk.

Everyone thought he was crazy for wanting to build a chocolate factory in the middle of prime Pennsylvania farmland without any major access to roads, a railway line, or even a town where factory workers could live. But Milton had already thought of the solutions to those problems. He'd build his own town, complete with a trolley system and railway.

There was only one major obstacle for him to overcome: He still needed a formula to produce milk chocolate. He built a lab across from his old homestead and, day and night, Milton and a few select workers labored to perfect a milk chocolate candy bar, like no other in the world.

Hershey's lab where he created his famous milk chocolate bar.

Hershey's chocolate factory. Notice the Hershey's Kiss lamp post. *Courtesy of Cindy Wolf*

Hershey was very busy building his chocolate empire, but he still found the time to pursue a personal life. He married a woman named Catherine Sweeney. She was nicknamed Kitty, and she and Milton were very happy together. The only downside to their relationship was that Kitty had a recurring illness that limited her travel at times. But, that barely stopped her and Milton from taking time to travel all over the world.

After two years of constant construction, the Hershey Chocolate Factory was complete. It was the world's largest chocolate factory, and was the real-world rival of the fictional Willie Wonka. The factory was also unique in construction in that it didn't have any windows in the building. Milton Hershey, felt that windows were a distraction for workers and he wanted his factory to run as efficiently as possible. As Milton Hershey's company grew, it became the world's first nationally-marketed chocolate company. Hershey realized he needed to house all the workers and their families, but he didn't want to build a dreary factory town like so many of his other industrialist contemporaries had built. He wanted a town that felt like home. He wanted his workers to *want* to live there. He wanted to create his version of a utopia community, complete with tree-lined streets, a park, and an inexpensive public transportation system.

When his good friend, Harry Liebkicker, unveiled the plans for the town to him, Hershey was outraged! They hadn't listened to him at all. He yelled that the houses looked like slave quarters from before the Civil War. Putting his foot down, he ordered new plans for the town and fired Liebkicker as project manager.

The result is the town of Hershey as we see it today. Milton Hershey, didn't stop just at building nice houses and an adequate transportation system. No, he also wanted to provide top-notch recreation facilities because he knew the more comfortable and happy his employees were, the more productive they would be for him.

On April 24, 1907, Hersheypark opened with the playing of a baseball game. They played on the new field under the amused eyes of Milton and Kitty Hershey who watched it along with the rest of the town from the grandstand.

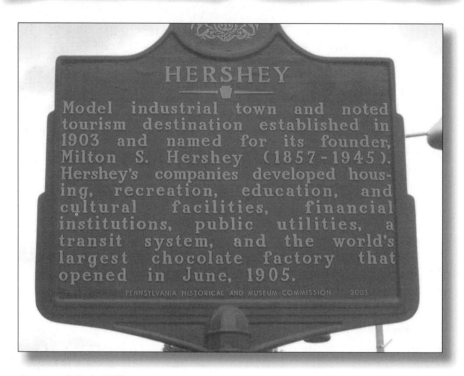

HERSHEY

Model industrial town and noted tourism destination established in 1903 and named for its founder, Milton S. Hershey (1857-1945). Hershey's companies developed housing, recreation, education, and cultural facilities, financial institutions, public utilities, a transit system, and the world's largest chocolate factory that opened in June, 1905.

PENNSYLVANIA HISTORICAL AND MUSEUM COMMISSION   2003

Courtesy of Cindy Wolf

Over the next decade, more attractions would be added to the park: roller coasters and other amusement rides such as a carousel, a swimming pool, and a grand ballroom. Once word got out, not just local workers were using the park, thousands of out-of-towners were visiting the park as well. While Milton and the town of Hershey were enjoying success, the nation was heading for disaster. When the great depression hit, Milton Hershey, in his trademark fashion made a decision. He felt he had two choices. He could cut back on expenses and fire people, and then end up supporting them on welfare, or, start what he called his "Great Building Project," to provide jobs for the 600 builders who lived in the community. Since building supplies were at an all-time low cost, it was in a easy choice for Hershey to make: start building.

Milton Hershey suffered the worst tragedy of his life in 1915. His beloved wife, Kitty, died prematurely as a result of her life-long illness. Before she had died, Kitty had given Milton the idea to establish a school for orphaned boys, since they were unable to have children of their own because of Kitty's illness. He and Kitty agreed to call it the Hershey Industrial School, which was later changed to the name Milton S. Hershey School. Three years after the death of Kitty, Milton secretly endowed the school the entire stock of the Hershey Company, setting the growth and continued welfare of the students as one of his highest priorities.

Hershey never remarried and spent the rest of his life committed to making the quality of life for his workers and the quality products of his company a priority.

The town of Hershey, Pennsylvania, is still a special place for the people who live and work there. It's still a popular place for millions of people to visit each year. Hershey really isn't a town— not officially anyway. There's no Mayor or town council. It's part of Derry Township, but that doesn't stop people from still calling it home. And where there's a home, there's usually a ghost story or two lurking around the corner. Hershey and the surrounding area is no exception.

Chapter Two
The Hershey Theater

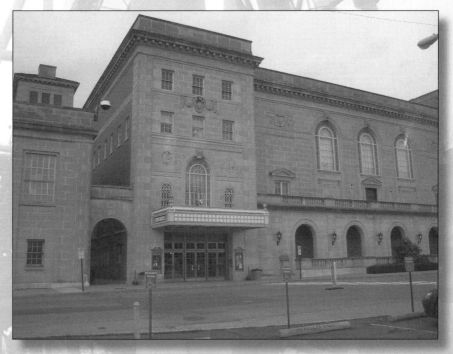

Does the spirit of Milton Hershey still haunt the catacombs beneath the Hershey Theater? *Courtesy of Cindy Wolf*

Milton Hershey wanted his town to be a cultural center for his workers. He had built a community center and part of this center was built as a theater. The Hershey Theater is actually part of the larger structure called the Hershey Community Building.

It was completed in 1933, the same year as the Hotel Hershey. The Community Building was built by the same architect as the Hotel Hershey as part of Milton Hershey's great building project. The building sits in the heart of the town of Hershey, directly across the street from the chocolate factory. It's a magnificent five-story structure that covers a whopping six acres. Housed inside the community building is a dining room, cafeteria for the chocolate factory workers, a library, offices, a recreational center, and most of all, the Hershey Theater. The entire right wing of the community building is occupied by the 2,000-seat theater.

When entering the lobby, be prepared to be awed by the detailed frescoes on the walls and the ceiling in the classical Greek style in blue and gold hues.

Once you get over the eye candy in the lobby, you'll leave to enter the main theater. Here, you'll think you've entered the courtyard of a Renaissance-style Venetian Castle. The seats are plushly upholstered and there really is no such thing as a bad seat

Milton Hershey's favorite seat: T-27.

in the house. Milton Hershey's favorite seat was T-27, down in the orchestra seating section towards the front of the theater.

When the curtain is down, the scene of a Venetian Canal, complete with gondolas, castles, and the famous Doge's palace, finishes the scene.

Inside the Proscenium Arch, there used to be a statue of Saint Mark, but sometime in the past, it went missing and no one has been able to find it to put it in its proper place. The walls on either side of the theater are built to look like facades, cleverly representing the outside of a Byzantine Castle complete with a windowed tower and golden battlements overhead.

The ceiling is an ever-changing display of clouds one minute and then a midnight sky of a thousand twinkling stars the next.

The Hershey Theater's stage illuminated such stars over the years as Roy Rogers, Blackstone and the magician, David Copperfield, and many others. Each year, the theater hosts traveling shows such as, *Momma Mia*, *Spamalot* and other Broadway shows.

On the day I chose to investigate the theater, they were giving what they call a Spotlight Tour. The informative, hour-long tour takes you behind the stage and into the underground catacombs beneath the theater.

It was perfect for my ghost hunting information gathering. The tour was very thorough and as we walked outside and around the Community Building, I took many pictures with my digital camera without a problem.

When we went inside is when I started experience problems with my camera. As we sat in the theater proper, listening to the guide from our seats in the orchestra section, my camera started beeping that the battery was low. Not possible, I thought, I'd just charged all the batteries before I left home that morning and had only taken a fraction of pictures on the outside of the building. Certainly not enough to have drained the battery, and besides, it was a bright sunny day outside and I didn't even use the flash. But there in front of me was a low battery icon flashing. I quickly popped out the depleted battery and inserted a fresh new one. I checked the setting on my camera to make sure that the battery was fully charged and proceeded to join the rest of my tour group as we headed to the stage area for the next part of our tour.

I've had the problem with the camera at other haunted locations. It seems that spirits feed on electromagnetic energy and one of their favorite snacks is the battery pack in digital cameras or camcorders.

So far, I hadn't gotten any paranormal evidence on film, but there was much, much more of the tour to complete.

Our next stop was backstage. The Hershey Theater's stage is huge, although from the audience view point it doesn't seem that big. The stage is seventy feet wide by forty-one feet deep. After giving our group the chance to stand in the spotlight, so to speak, we migrated to the upper level of the theater and had a chance to view the stage from the balcony seating area.

This is where things get a little crazy. I had just taken my seat and noticed that again, to my surprise, the camera was blinking

A picture of the orchestra seating area. Notice the ectoplasmic orb in the upper left corner.

Notice the orb between the two heads.

With all the orbs floating around the theater, it's no wonder my camera batteries were drained!

that it was on low battery. I took a few snapshots of the theater trying to encompass the overall view of the castle-like interior and managed to catch quite a few of, what are known as, orbs floating in the theater.

Some ghost hunters are skeptical at best of the validity of orbs and feel that they are either: A) insects, B) dust, or C) undetermined electromagnetic energy, that may or may not prove a location is haunted. Most of the time, it is hard to tell the difference between the three.

Well, for starters, I was inside and hardly felt that the Hershey Theater had insects flying around, so I ruled out the insect theory. As for dust, it was an old theater and could quite possibly be dusty, but it should have been dusty on every floor, not just the second floor, and when I took pictures in the lower orchestra area, I didn't capture dust or orbs in any of those pictures. So if it was dust, it would have been in *all* of the pictures and not just *some* of the pictures. Ultimately, I'm left with letter C explanation: undetermined electromagnetic energy.

Most ghost hunters choose to either play it safe and dismiss them or be just accept that they could very well be paranormal in nature. I'm just recording what I've noticed and will let you decide for yourself.

My second battery was almost out of charge and it had only been about twenty minutes since I'd put in fresh batteries. I hadn't taken that many pictures. I use this same camera on vacation and snap at least several dozen pictures, even with using the flash before the battery would start to lose its charge. Here, in the theater, I had shot at best maybe two dozen pictures before I'd had to change the batteries not once, but twice. Reluctantly, I popped out a battery once again and replaced it with my third and final battery.

We left the balcony, proceeded to the projection room, and then marched down a steep staircase to the basement of the theater. Allowing everyone else to go ahead of me, I followed at the rear just so I could take some pictures without crowds of people around. The catacombs of the basement of the theater are what you would expect, cramped dark and twisty.

This orb photo was captured in the basement.

Small dressing rooms and supply rooms lined either side of the weaving corridors and are marked in spray paint signaling how to get to stage right or stage left. It was down here that I had held back from the group to take some pictures by myself.

A particular side corridor seemed to beckon me, although I can't explain why. That is until I took a close look at the pictures I shot down there. I took two pictures of the same dressing room, and in one of the pictures, there is nothing out of the ordinary, just a room, but in the other, there is a bright glowing orb! Both pictures were snapped at the same angle and with the same flash. The one has a brightly-colored orb in the center and the other does not. I'm at a loss to explain it.

The guide ended the tour back in the main theater and the first row next to the stage. One of the great features of the tour was a close look at the classic 78 rank Aeolian-Skinner organ that was installed when the theater was built and is only played at certain times, such as prior to the classical film series and other concert events.

When the other tourists left, I questioned the tour guide with my usual first question. So are there any ghost stories associated with the Hershey theater? Disappointingly, she didn't know any of them, but here's where the interesting part comes. She led me to where a few of the employees of the theater were eating lunch and some of them were gracious enough to take some time out of their lunch break to enlighten me about some of the tales of the 75-year-old theater.

Many of the people who have worked in the theater have had some strange experiences over the years. One of these people, Millie Morsis, has shed some light on one of the most persistent mysteries in recent years—the mystery of the Phantom typist. For over twenty years, various workers have heard the sound of an antique typewriter echoing through the lobby and orchestra seating area. According to Ms. Morsis, you could hear at any time of the day or night the sounds of tapping on the keys of an old typewriter. Sometimes this would be very loud and at other times it would be very faint. "You can hear the tapping quite clearly," she explained. "Sometimes you'd hear it during a very quiet moment during a classical concert." She explained further, "We really thought we had some sort of annoying phantom typist who didn't know when to quit typing during a performance. Everyone who worked here has heard it some time or another."

It was during the renovations in 2003 and 2004 that the mystery of the phantom was finally, and disappointingly, solved. Ms. Morsis and her co-workers were sad to find out that their resident ghost of over twenty years turned out to be a window in the upper foyer area that was warped and would rattle at the slightest breeze, while making the sound of an old typewriter's keys clacking at the hands of a spectral typist.

After the workers fixed the window, the sound was never heard again. Leave it to modernization to kill a ghost!

That's not to say that the old theater doesn't harbor a real specter, though. According to another theater employee, one of the other tour guides told her that a tourist taking the Spotlight tour

This balcony door turned out to be the Phantom Typist of the Hershey Theater. *Courtesy of Cindy Wolf*

had complained of smelling cigar smoke down in the catacombs beneath the theater. The tourist mentioned it to the tour guide who told the person that there was no smoking allowed in the theater. No one else, including the tour guide, smelled anything at the time. It's well known that Milton Hershey always enjoyed a good cigar. Could he be dividing his afterlife time between the Hotel Hershey and the Hershey theater. Why not? He must have plenty of time on his hands.

To visit the Hershey Theater, go southeast on Park Avenue/ PA 743 towards West Chocolate Avenue/US 422, then turn left onto West Chocolate Avenue/ 743 south, turn right onto Cocoa Avenue/PA 743, then left onto East Caracas Avenue. The Hershey Theater is located at 15 Caracas Avenue and is open for tours only on certain days of the week throughout the year.

Chapter 3
Ghosts of the Park

The entrance to Hersheypark. Notice the life-size bronze statue of Milton Hershey and the haunted carousel in the background. *Courtesy of Cindy Wolf*

Milton Hershey always wanted to build a nice park and recreation area for his workers and their families. Lucky for us visitors to the park, Milton chose not to listen to his mother who thought his idea was far too frivolous and unnecessary. Her opinion didn't stop her from enjoying shows at the park's outdoor amphitheater when it was built later, though.

The park's original appeal was that it was a great spot to picnic and a stroll through graceful trees and wooded areas without feeling crowded. On April 24, 1907, Hersheypark officially opened with a baseball game. Over the years, many enhancements were added to the park; one of the earliest additions has a reputation for being haunted: The Carousel.

In July of 1912, Hersheypark acquired a new, magnificent, and the most modern carousel in the eastern part of the United States. It was called P.T.C. # 41, and was originally located along Spring Creek. The carousel was fifty feet in diameter and featured fifty-three animals, including brightly-painted pigs, rabbits, lions, ostrich, deer, goats, bears, and two large ornate chariots, not to mention horses. Further enhancing the riding experience, it had a Wurlitzer band organ installed. The carousel was the pride of an already beautiful park and reigned supreme in the same spot for nearly fifty years.

Then, in 1971, the park underwent a massive redevelopment project that was to turn it from a small regional park into the world-class theme park it is today. The carousel, was dismantled and renovated for an entire year. On May 7, 1972, it was rebuilt

Is this carousel haunted? *Courtesy of Cindy Wolf*

and rededicated in its new location at Carousel Circle and has been there ever since.

It seems that all the hauntings of the park started when they were doing renovations. This isn't unusual. Many times, when people begin renovating an old house, it starts a series of paranormal events. Could the same have happened to an old amusement park?

Picture Hersheypark as it is today: Laughter, screams of excitement, and the roar of the crowds as roller coasters zoom by are what most people are greeted with as they enter Hersheypark. And it's no wonder. Hersheypark is filled with whooshing, flashing roller coasters, and colorful characters depicting favorite confections invented by Milton Hershey over a hundred years ago.

In fact, in 2008, the park celebrated 100 years of Happy, and to mark the landmark occasion, a new section was added. The all-American boardwalk, to hearken back to the olden days when the park first opened to the public.

After the last guest has left the park and the music and fun has faded into the darkness, the park takes on a totally different atmosphere. Once the many colorful lights are turned off for the night and only the security lighting illuminates the park, the once cheerful facades of the rides and buildings seem a bit more foreboding and almost sinister. Skeletal roller coaster rails glisten with the moonlight like the bones of a serpent. Kiosks and vending buildings cast dense shadows over twisting walkways. It's not by chance that places like these feel more frightening in the dark. When theaters and parks and malls are empty of crowds of people, they almost seem as though they themselves are ghosts.

Imagine you're a security guard making your rounds to insure the park is secure for the night. It's nerve racking just thinking that a person could easily catch you off guard, but when you walk round the park at that time of the night who knows what tricks your mind might play on you. The park has many places that a potential trespasser, or trespassers, could hide.

Suddenly, out of the corner of your eye you spot movement over by the carousel. It looks like a figure moving around to the

The Comet rollercoaster. A phantom figure has been spotted at night here.

opposite side. You quickly move towards the 1912-era contraption to get a better look at whatever, or whoever, might be there before calling in an alert. A chill creeps across the back of your neck as you tighten your jacket round your shoulders, more for support than from actually being cold. Your hands grip your flashlight as you cautiously head in the direction of the shadowy figure.

Of course you've heard all the stories from the other guards about how Mr. Hershey's ghost has been sighted in the park checking up on things, but you've never believed them, until now. Casting your flashlight over the area shows nothing. You radio back to the security center. Did anything show up on the security cameras? Your coworkers says, "No, why, have you seen someone?"

"No reason, just checking," you reply. You continue on through the route, and you swear someone is in the shadows watching, as you walk past the classic Comet rollercoaster. Is that the sound of footsteps echoing on the wooden structure? Someone is running inside the waiting area!

Again, you radio to the security room. No one is showing up on the security camera you're told. You decide to go and check it out anyway. Casting your light over the area shows nothing. Cautiously, you shine your light on the loading area of the rollercoaster—nothing and no one. Just as you're was about to go somewhere else, you flash your light over a piece of the track, and your jaw just about drops. You see the impossible—someone climbing the maintenance stairs near the first incline.

The translucent figure seems unconcerned with a light shining on it and continues to climb.

That's enough for you, and you decide to return to the security center for a break and a nice calming cup of coffee.

The previous story has happened to numerous security personnel, so the stories goes. But the *official* story from the security office inside the old Hershey Stadium is that nothing paranormal has occurred in the park. What do *you* think?

A frequent story passed among park employees is the story of a maintenance worker who was servicing a rollercoaster called

Is the Super Dooper Looper under a curse?

The Super Duper Looper. The looping roller coaster, has a fifty-seven-foot high loop! It was built in 1976 and was the first looping roller coaster built on the East Coast. It was the park's most expensive ride costing three million dollars, could carry twenty-four passengers and is 1,614 feet long.

The rollercoaster was designed by Anton Schwartzkopf of West Germany. The question: Is the Super Duper Looper cursed? When it was unveiled to the public on media day in 1977, in front of every media reporter radio and television crew from the surrounding area, several company executives and their family members were to take the first public ride. When the train left the loading area and ascended to the top of the first hill, it inexplicably stopped. In spite of the efforts of the maintenance crew, they couldn't get the ride started and all the passengers had to climb down an access ladder. Ghostly or mechanical?

The most reoccurring ghost story is that of the maintenance worker who died while working on the Super Duper Looper. I was only about twelve years old at the time this happened, but I remember my parents commenting on the news about the worker being killed. According to the story, he was at the bottom of the first hill where the steel track curves upward into the fifty-seven-foot loop. He was working on the electrical wiring and had accidentally crossed two wires, which in turn activated the break release of the car at the top. Somehow he didn't notice that train coming until it was fatally too late...

According to all accounts, the ride broke down so often that it drew enormous resources and was very frustrating. In fact, the rollercoaster needed repairs so often, they had to rebuild the lift system to the top of the first hill.

The question remains: Was it simply a mechanical problem or was there something more supernatural involved? Could the ghost of the maintenance man have been sabotaging the very ride that took his life? We will probably never know.

Could this be where the track maintenance worker died?

The Ghost Children of the Hershey Swimming Pool

According to park employees, there is a rumor that several children drowned in the pool, located across the street from the rear of Chocolate World. The only remnant of the once heavily-attended pool is the lighthouse that is next to the road, and a large flat area. The swimming pool was built in 1929 along Spring Creek consisting of four pools and a bathhouse. The cost to build such an elaborate structure has been estimated at $100,000 and included a bathhouse made of stucco and brick in the Spanish and Moroccan style—not unlike the main lobby of the Hotel Hershey.

It officially opened on Saturday, July 13, 1929. There was an older pool as well, built in 1910 with a bathhouse and a 40-foot-high, 100-foot-long water slide. As of now, these ghost children have been reportedly seen in the flat open area behind Chocolate World by some park employees. They've mainly been spotted late

This lighthouse and field are all that remain of the old Hersheypark swimming pool.

at night or very early in the morning when no children should be anywhere near the park, let alone wearing old-fashioned bathing suits and carrying beach towels.

Milton Hershey was known to allow the boys from his school to visit the pool in the summer. Could some of these ghostly children be his students?

The Moaning Woman

During the 1970s, the park underwent a major expansion. One of the biggest and boldest changes was the enclosure of the whole park and a charging overall admission. Not everyone who lived in and around Hershey was happy with this development. Many people thought the park should remain open with free admission.

This is where the sad woman's spirit has been heard by several park employees

The redevelopment over a five-year period called for many changes in the park. Adding new rides and a new entrance celebrating the German heritage of the local population were just a few of the changes made.

The west side of the park needed to be expanded to make room for more space. This required that all of the homes on Derry Road that were west of Park Avenue had to be destroyed. A majority of the homes were owned by the Hershey estate. The problem was that not all of them were.

Amanda Knoll is a former Hersheypark employee and manager of the building near the Kissing Tower. She advised that the building across from the Kissing Tower was used for several different purposes over the years, including a storage vault, a Chinese Food stand, and most recently a Boardwalk Fries stand. According to park employees' legend, on the site stood a house where the longtime-owner refused sell her property to the Hershey Company. According to several different sources, the woman was pressured into selling her home against her will and became depressed over losing her home. She ultimately committed suicide in the upstairs attic of the house.

Many people who work in the building that used to be this woman's former house have heard moaning and wailing that sounds like a woman in pain. The female voice comes from the upstairs storage area of the building. No one has ever *seen* anyone, but could this poor person's unhappy ending of life have caused her to remain behind? The area where people hear this moaning is known as "the loft." I've never been able to find any evidence that this incident happened, but sometimes these unpleasant tales have a way of surfacing in strange ways.

To get to Hersheypark, go north on Park Avenue/PA 743 towards Trinidad Avenue, then turn left onto Hersheypark Drive.

Chapter Four
The Hotel Hershey

In 1933, thirty years after the founding of the town of Hershey, Milton Hershey decided it was time for his town to have a big impressive hotel, one that would rival some of the finest hotels in New York, London, and Paris. Unlike other wealthy industrialists,

Several sightings of Milton and Kitty Hershey's spirits have occurred at the Hotel Hershey. Courtesy of Cindy Wolf

Milton decided to embark on a great community building project at the time when most businesses were cutting back because of the great depression.

Milton Hershey gave thousands of people jobs during this time and the town of Hershey flourished when other factory towns were becoming literal ghost towns.

The Hotel Hershey sits high atop the town of Hershey on Prospect Heights, which was originally known as Pat's Hill. Paul Witmer, the architect of the hotel, was pulled off the job of constructing the massive Community Building in downtown Hershey to work on the hotel. By the early part of 1933, the four-story-high building, constructed of glazed brick, dominated the countryside for miles around.

To this day, the Hotel Hershey is a perfect example of a structure in the old Spanish tradition architecture and atmosphere. But then nothing built by Hershey would have you expect anything less than opulence and style. Milton Hershey fully embraced the saying: "Go big or go home!"

For example, you won't find a conventional lobby at the Hotel Hershey. Instead, you'll walk into what appears to be an outside tiled courtyard patio in a Spanish villa, complete with a center tiled fountain and a ceiling painted to look like the Tuscany sky.

As beautiful and elegantly decorated as the Hotel Hershey is, the guests are reluctant to leave, and according to some of the stories there, it may be that some of them have decided to return from the afterlife.

Al Rossi, a forty-year veteran employee at the Hotel Hershey was kind enough to point me in the direction of two wonderful ladies who work in the housekeeping department of the Hotel, and while he himself didn't have any ghost stories about the hotel, he assured me that these women would—and was he right!

The ladies, between the two of them had almost thirty years experience working at the Hotel Hershey. And they had stories. Lots of stories about the paranormal side of the hotel. I had just hoped I would have enough paper copy notes of all the information.

We sat down in one of the grand side lobbies of the hotel and they were gracious enough to sacrifice some of their break time to clue me in to some of the more famous incidents that happened over the years at the old hotel. When one of them had run out stories to tell, the other woman would suddenly jog her memories and come up with another story.

We were sitting on the fifth floor of the hotel and the self-proclaimed "Misfits" of the housekeeping staff started their tales of haunting there. On the fifth floor, there is a stockroom that the cleaning staff uses to keep supplies in. It's a fairly large walk-in room. Many members of the staff have had strange feelings in the room, as if they were being watched, and many times they would feel a chilling in the room or detect the odor of cigar smoke. Considering the hotel is smoke-free and smoking in an enclosed room in a non-designated area could get them fired, most of the staff who have experienced this have no explanation, or at least no rational explanation.

Milton Hershey always used to enjoy smoking a good Cuban cigar, so most of the employees think it's old Milton keeping a watchful eye on them.

Like most haunted buildings, the Hotel Hershey has its share of strange unexplained noises. One of the Misfits told me about her encounter in the fifth floor hallway. It seems that, at one time, the towers that you can see from the outside of the hotel were accessible from the inside. But back in the 1970s, when the hotel was being renovated, they decided to seal them off. While working near the wall, cleaning, she heard the sound of someone walking up a metal staircase. That in itself wouldn't be anything out of the ordinary unless you take into account the fact that the only metal staircase was inside the tower that had been sealed up for the last thirty plus years!

She claims she distinctly heard the sound of heavy work boots on the metal stairs. She asked at the office if they knew of anyone who was inside the towers working and was told that the towers hadn't been unsealed for any reason. So she just went back to work, and chalked it up to just another strange day at the Hotel Hershey.

Phantom footsteps have been heard inside this tower. *Courtesy of Cindy Wolf*

On the second floor, in one of the rooms in the 200s in the East Wing, a cleaning person would hear the sound of a female laughing and mumbling. At the time this person heard the sounds, no one was to be in that area of the building. This cleaning person was also a very conscientious cleaner and many times, when she would go to those rooms to clean, objects would not be as she left them only moments before.

Kitty Hershey, or someone who greatly resembles her, has been spotted on the ninth floor by the other half of the Misfits cleaning staff. Llenay, a ten-year veteran employee of the hotel would notice movement out of the corner of her eye while she was changing linens in rooms on the ninth floor. This had gone on for some time and she was determined to get to the bottom of who was there. No other staff was on that floor in the early morning hours. That wing was her assigned area. Finally, after feeling that she was being watched while cleaning room 916 she looked out into the hallway and saw a hazy, gray female dressed

The room where Kitty Hershey's spirit was seen walking past.

The ninth floor hallway where a gray female spirit has been sighted.

in clothing from the 1800s, early 1900s, and wearing a big floppy hat in that same era style. The figure walked (or glided) past her cart and continued down the hall, or so she thought. In the few seconds it took her to recover, she ran to the door and looked past her cart down the hall where the figure was heading. There was no one there and no place for anyone to hide. The woman simply vanished into thin air.

The hallways of the Hotel Hershey twist and turn and are very winding. Except on the ninth floor. That is one of the straighter hallways in the hotel and also one of the smallest. The room where Llenay spotted the female specter was right before the elevator lobby on that floor. It is very easy to see around the corner, and if anyone was playing a prank on her that day, it would have been very difficult to disappear as she stated the figure did. There is an access stairway near the door but it is easily spotted from the hall and the room.

Kitty Hershey's spirit also has a fascination with elevators. Many times employees of the hotel will use the elevators and find that they won't work properly, such as the doors refusing to close or won't open on the correct floor. Llenay says that usually when that happens they have to ask Kitty to stop playing with the elevators. They inexplicably start working again.

Not to be left out M.S. Hershey likes to make his presence known to the hotel staff in a variety of ways. During the reconstruction of the hotel, in the mid 1970s, a man matching the description of M.S. Hershey was sighted one early spring morning by some of the staff of the hotel. He was dressed in a business suit in the style of early 1900s, wearing a top hat and—here's the clincher—smoking a cigar as he stood on an outdoor patio and looked out upon the town of Hershey. This was a restricted area and the staff person reported it to the on-duty supervisor who had Security do a search, but, not surprisingly, no one matching that description was ever found in the area. It couldn't have been any of the construction workers because none of them had arrived to work yet.

A few years ago, a family with a seven-year-old daughter was staying at the Hotel Hershey. According to several different hotel staff members, the story goes that the girl woke up in the middle of the night terrified that there was an intruder in her room. She pointed to her bathroom and said there was an old man standing in the doorway watching her. Her parents thoroughly checked the room and found no intruder, old or otherwise. They chalked it up to the girl having a nightmare from sleeping in a strange room. They tucked her back in bed and went back to sleep.

The next day the family was going to Hersheypark as planned, the incident of the night before long forgotten by the parents in preparing for the days adventure. En route to the main entrance to the amusement park, the family decided to stop to visit Chocolate World.

Chocolate World was the answer to the Hershey Foods Corporation's many requests to tour the chocolate factory. Years ago, the public was able to tour the actual manufacturing plant

The third floor, where Milton Hershey's spirit frightened a little girl.

where the chocolate bars were processed. But, the plant tour was so popular that it was disrupting work. People would wait in long lines to tour the plant, and traffic, (always a problem), would be worse when the tours were given. The solution was to build a separate building with a simulation of a chocolate

factory. Chocolate World opened its doors in 1973, allowing large numbers of people to ride a simulation ride depicting how chocolate bars are made.

Also in Chocolate World there are a large number of pictures of Milton Hershey scattered throughout the complex. One of these portraits of the founder caught the little girls eye. "That's him!" she cried. "That's who was watching me in my room last night...from the bathroom!"

Her parents didn't know what to say. They knew she wasn't making it up because this was the first time she had ever been to Hershey and had never made anything up like this before.

Perhaps, the spirit of M.S. Hershey was just looking out for the little girl and was caught by surprise. All we know is that this happened in room 315 at the Hotel Hershey. So if you ever have a child that stays in that room, or any other for that matter, and they wake you up in the middle of the night, don't be so sure to dismiss their fears. It just might be old Milton checking up on them before a big day at his park.

On a recent trip to the Hotel Hershey with my nephew, Douglas, we attempted to take some photos of the haunted areas of the hotel. Without exception, every time I tried to take a picture of either a haunted room or a haunted hallway, there was a problem with the camera. Several pictures came out distorted and blurry as if the camera had been shaken (which it was not!). Other times it came out as a double image especially room number 315. The second and third floor hallways were the worst distortion, but there was some on the ninth floor as well.

During the 1970s, a bartender got quite frightened the time he went down to the old wine cellar to retrieve stock for his bar.

He was always leery of going down to that dank, dark, dimly-lit room by himself, but he needed to be ready for the crowd of hotel patrons who would be frequenting the hotel bar that night. Cautiously, he made his way down the creaky, wooden steps. He made sure that he would find just what he needed and then quickly leave.

Problem was, it wasn't so easy to find things down there. After all, the wine cellar was over thirty years old and was hand picked by Mr. Hershey himself, a fine purveyor of wine. He started looking for what he needed, and the whole time he was down there, it felt as though he was being watched. The hairs on the back of his neck prickled and his ears perked up.

Clink! One of the bottles behind him in the wine rack had just rattled. *Okay,* he thought, *nothing to be upset about. Bottles shift from time to time. Maybe someone from another shift didn't put it back correctly.*

Clink, rattle, clack! Another few bottles moved! Now he was starting to get nervous. Then another bottle rattled, and then another; he started to sweat. So, all the bottles were rattling and shaking. That was enough for him! He grabbed what he'd found so far and quickly dashed for the stairs and closing the cellar door with slam.

It was only then that the other thing that had bothered him while he was down there by himself came to mind. The smell of cigar smoke! There was only one person who used to smoke cigars down in that room and he'd been dead for more than thirty years! Milton Hershey!

To get to the Hotel Hershey, go north on Park Avenue/PA 743 towards Trinidad Avenue. Cross over Hersheypark Drive and go straight on Sand Beach Road, turn left onto Front Street, and then turn right onto Hotel Road.

Chapter 5
The Ghosts of Cloverdale

Milton Hershey always claimed that the idea for starting a school for orphaned boys was Kitty Hershey's idea. As mentioned earlier, they were both fond of children, but because of Kitty's illness, they would never be able to have children of their own.

The Homestead, where the students first lived.

In the early 1900s, Milton and Kitty realized that they had more wealth than they knew what to do with. Even after expanding the chocolate factory and taking long trips to foreign countries, they still had more to spend. Kitty made the suggestion that they spend the money on children who were less fortunate than others and also suggested building an orphanage for them.

Milton thought it was a very good idea but wanted to take it one step further. He suggested not only building an orphanage, but building a whole school system that those less advantaged boys could learn a valuable trade that would help them later on in life long after they left the school. Milton told her: "Let them earn their own livings."

It was on November 15, 1909, that the Hersheys deeded 486 acres of prime Pennsylvania farmland in nearby Hershey, Pennsylvania, in the vicinity of his old homestead, to the Hershey Trust Company which is now housed in his old mansion called High Point. The Trust company was to be the trustee of the newly-formed Hershey Industrial School that was to be located in the area of Derry Township.

The document stated that the school was to be used as a home for boys who had lost one or both parents. The first two boys admitted to the school were from Mount Joy, Pennsylvania. Later, two more boys from nearby were brought to the school. Boys from Lebanon, Harrisburg, and Lancaster were all admitted to the school in the early years, all of them having suffered a story of tragedy. At first, for a number of years, the boys lived and learned at the Homestead, but as the Hersheys soon found out, there would soon be a need for expansion, because there were many more boys attending the school than planned for initially.

They lived on the ancestral homestead of Milton Hershey, built from chunks of limestone from the fields where Milton Hershey eventually chose to build his chocolate factory.

Obviously, Milton and Kitty Hershey were unable to oversee the day-to-day activities of the school. In fact, Kitty Hershey was so ill in 1914, she seldom went to the school as it was very difficult for her to walk any distance. Milton Hershey on the other hand, visited every week.

The Hersheys assigned a man named George Copenhaver and his wife, Prudence, to be in charge of the school.

Over the years, the Hershey Industrial School gained so many students that it had to be moved out of the Homestead. At first, they used an old cattle barn converted into a schoolroom, but as the student numbers grew, up to 1,100 at one pointm they soon realized that the homestead and the cow barn classroom would soon be outgrown.

Gradually, one a farmland after another was bought and added to the growing school property. Even as busy as Hershey was tending to his chocolate business and an ailing wife, he still kept in close touch with everything that went on in the school. He even traveled to New York City to ask other school administrators at the Russell Sage Foundation for advice, as well as to Philadelphia to see the school that Steven Gerard had founded. Hershey took many of his ideas for his foundation document from the Gerard Foundation because he wanted to be sure that no one would be able to interfere with the funds for his school, with the exception of his wife, Kitty, and himself.

In 1915, one of the most tragic, if not the most tragic, event in Milton Hershey life took place. After her long illness, Kitty Hershey finally died in a hotel in Philadelphia, after visiting a number of specialist doctors and going to many faraway Health Resorts. Milton Hershey was devastated and grief stricken. It was then, unbeknown to attorneys and Hershey Company executives, that he decided to turn over most of his fortune to the school.

This time, Milton Hershey, fully threw himself into the project of expanding the school. He wanted to build a great school as a legacy of not only his life, but for his wife's vision that she so firmly believed in. He made a vow that their school would be the greatest school of its kind in the world.

Visit the school grounds today; you'll soon see that Milton Hershey kept his word. Not only did Hershey build one school building on the grounds, he built several.

He also started building separate housing units for the students to live in. Each housing building has its own set of house parents to oversee the students. One of these houses, called Cloverdale, may have some residents that aren't on the school roster.

As much as the boys who lived in the school were grateful for the opportunity to better themselves, at least one of them couldn't get over his family tragedy and hung himself in the attic of the Cloverdale house. Although this was never confirmed, no one hasn't been able to debunk the rumor either.

According to the son of the house parents in Cloverdale, his mother and one of the students were alone in the house. They distinctly heard the sound of footsteps running down the stairs, then running back up the stairs and slamming the door on the upper floor of the house. The mother and student heard the noise while they were sitting in the kitchen. Apparently, the sound frightened the female student so much that she ran out of the house.

When the husband arrived home he searched the house, but no intruders were ever found. After the incident on the stairs, the house mother had another encounter with the supernatural. All of the students were at their homes away from Hershey, for vacation. She was doing a random check of the rooms to make sure that they were clean. It was dark, and as she walked down the dim hallway, she felt the grip of a hand fall down on her shoulder from behind. She wheeled around thinking it was her husband sneaking up on her in the dark, but no one was there. There were no rooms for someone to have ducked into quickly, just the walls of the hall to either side of her.

For some reason known only to them, there are spirits that have a fascination with closets and doors. I've read accounts in other ghost lore books about how certain doors won't stay shut or won't be able to be opened. Perhaps because doorways act as a portal from one room to another, they might also function as a secondary purpose as a portal for spirits to manifest themselves.

At Cloverdale, the family and students had an upstairs closet door that refused to stay shut. People would shut the door, walk into another room, and come back to find that the closet door was open again. Students who stayed in the house would also try to shut and lock the closet door with no luck. They tried locking the door and putting boxes in front of the door. It would stay closed as long as someone was in room, but as soon as someone left the room they would find the door back open again. No explanation was ever found for why this kept happening.

Another phenomenon prevalent in haunted houses is electrical equipment turning itself on and off. Sometimes, its the lights; at other times, it will be the television; and in one instance, there was even a report of a toilet that would constantly flush by itself throughout the night. According to the house parents' son, one of the weirdest things to be encountered was in the basement of the house. The basement was split into two separate rooms.

In the first room there was a ping-pong table and in the second room there was a small REC room area with a stereo system and television set. In order to get to the REC room, you had to walk through the ping-pong room. There was only one entrance to the room.

One night, when four people were playing ping-pong, the radio in the REC room came on by itself. They immediately ran to the REC room, and before that they could catch sight of the radio, it clicked off. When they inspected the stereo system, it was set to the tape recorder setting and should not have been playing the radio at all. No one could have been hiding in the room or could have slipped out the door without being seen by the other people in the ping-pong room.

The Hershey school grounds are always being upgraded and renovated. The Cloverdale house was remodeled, and according to the current people who live there, there hasn't been any paranormal activity lately.

To get to the Milton S. Hershey School, go southeast on Park Avenue/743 towards Chocolate Avenue/US 422, turn left onto West Chocolate Avenue/US 422 east/PA 743 South and then turn right onto Cocoa Avenue/PA743, turn left onto West Governor Road/US322, turn right onto Meadow Lane and turn right onto Spartan Lane.

Chapter 6

What if Mr. and Mrs. Hershey had died on the Titanic?

Milton and Kitty Hershey traveled in Europe extensively at times and they liked to travel in the lavish style very few people could afford. There is a copy of their tickets for passage on the ocean liner *Titanic* on display at the Hershey Museum. We know Hershey canceled his trip on the *Titanic* because of a business meeting. But what if the meeting had never occurred? How different would the town of Hershey be today if he and Kitty Hershey had died on that fateful day in 1912 on the *Titanic*. Consider this a ghost story of a future that very well could have happened.

One aspect of the Hershey legacy that would not have experienced much change would be the Hershey Industrial School for orphans. Milton Hershey had a deed of trust written in 1909 that was similar to the one created by Stephen Gerard in 1831, where he put into the deed at least 10,000 acres of property and the largest chunk of Hershey Company stock, making sure that the money would be used how they wished it, with no changes.

What was considered a gala fair in 1913, the tenth anniversary celebration of the founding of Hershey would have been quite different. Instead of a parade and fireworks, there would have probably been a somber memorial service. And the many speeches would have been praises and mourning of the early demise of the town's founder and his wife. The question is: Would the executors in charge of the Hershey chocolate company, after the death of Mr. Hershey, have built a town to the standards of Milton Hershey?

In 1916, Milton Hershey started a venture in Cuba. He had died in 1912, and it is unlikely that his remaining executives would have gone this route. William Murrie, a Hershey Company executive, was never very supportive of the Cuban enterprise. He was worried about the financial aspect being a burden on the company. It is unlikely that the executives would have thought the same about Cuba that Milton Hershey did, and in doing so, would have lost an advantage of having a large cheap sugar supply during the first world war.

Even though Milton S. Hershey and Kitty Hershey had made provisions for the school back in 1909, if they had died on the *Titanic* on its fateful maiden voyage, changes that Milton made in 1918, would never have happened. On November 13, Hershey secretly put every bit of his Hershey chocolate company stock into a trust for the industrial school. More than $60,000,000 worth— something the executives of the Hershey Company would never have done or even contemplated doing.

One good thing might have come out of an early demise of the Hershey's on the *Titanic*. In 1920, Milton Hershey made a disastrous financial error. He bought sugar contracts at a premium and failed to sell them when the price was quickly dropping. He was stuck holding expensive sugar contracts that he was forced to pay. But aside from the financial decisions, Milton Hershey also oversaw the development of his town and the park for the employees.

I think if Milton had died on the *Titanic*, the amusement park known as Hersheypark would not exist as it is today. Milton had a dream to make his park the leading amusement park in Central Pennsylvania, if not the United States. Had he not been around to make several early key decisions, it is doubtful that the park would have been developed into the grand amusement park.

The main point to understand about Hershey, Pennsylvania is that its founder, Milton Hershey had a very tight grip on the social and economic development of his factory town. He wanted to shape its future as a nice place to live and work. The park was meant to be an outlet for his employees to enjoy on a Sunday afternoon. It grew into a much more than that with direct involvement of Milton Hershey, a development that would have ended in a watery grave in 1912.

Many of the modern innovations that we take for granted today or considered a luxury back in the early twentieth century would also be affected. Milton Hershey felt that by making luxuries available to his workers, this made them more productive and happy with their lives. This in turn benefited his company by having fewer accidents and loss of work by his employees who worked very hard. If the Hersheys had died on the *Titanic* many of these luxuries never would have been built.

During the Great Depression, a lot of business were going bankrupt and others were cutting back on their workforce—thousands of people were unemployed. Milton Hershey, handled his affairs in an opposite fashion.

With his Great Building Plan, he not only kept his workers busy, he created hundreds of new jobs. Had he and Kitty died on the *Titanic*, it's very unlikely that the executives left in charge of the Hershey Company would have made the same decisions. The town of Hershey would not have built things like the theater, a community center, or a luxurious department store. The park would have been very basic and nothing like what developed in later years under this specific guidance of Milton Hershey.

The houses the people bought would probably have looked like other factory town houses—identical to one another, no luxuries like indoor plumbing, no greenery, and almost like slave quarters in a pre Civil War south. In fact, the first designer of the town of Hershey was rejected by Milton Hershey for that very reason. So, not only would the town of Hershey be a much more dismal place to live in, it would probably not be the tourist destination spot it is today. Many of the sites that people visit by the thousands each summer in Hershey, such as Hersheypark, the Hotel Hershey, and the Hershey Theater, would not exist as they are today, if not for Milton Hershey.

Milton Hershey wanted to build the Hotel Hershey much earlier than he did. But because of an error in judgment concerning a sugar contract he almost lost the company and was forced to put many building projects on hold. The Hotel Hershey was one of those projects. It's likely that a hotel would have been built on the site of the current Hotel Hershey, but would it have been as lavish and uniquely decorated? Probably not. Milton and Kitty Hershey had a close hand and deciding the decoration of the hotel most of it from their travels in Europe.

So the next time you visit Hershey, look around you. Think about how the history of this town would have changed, how different the ghosts would be, and how you personally would be affected, had Milton and Kitty kept their tickets for the great *Titantic* voyage.

Chapter 7

Eerie Ephrata

About half an hour drive to the east of Hershey. Lies the sleepy little town of Ephrata, Pennsylvania. Pronounced *capital F-rata*, with the emphasis on the *f*. The first town was founded in 1732 by a man named Johann Conrad Beissel. Beissel was a ne'er

All that remains of the original frontier commune are a few empty buildings at the Ephrata Cloisters.

do well Baker from Germany who had immigrated to the United States and had first lived in Philadelphia. He later had a vision where he moved outside the city and headed north to found a semi monastic order of seventh day Dunkers. He admitted both men and women, but they were a celibate order. Beissel started what is now called the Ephrata Cloisters and named after the Biblical town of Ephrath.

Many well-educated men and women belonged to this order, including a man known as Peter Miller, who at the request of the continental Congress translated the Declaration of Independence into seven languages.

The Ephrata Cloister literally carved a civilization out of the wilderness and was a tower of learning. At its peak of prosperity, there were nearly 300 men and women living in the community. They had a working sawmill, paper mill, a printing press, and various other industries.

The town of Ephrata grew around the community of the cloisters. There's even a Revolutionary war connection to the town. From a small start of a monastic community of 300, the town has grown today in population to over 13,000—and so have their ghosts.

Ghosts of the Revolutionary War...In Ephrata?

Most people associate the Revolutionary War with places such as Philadelphia, Williamsburg, Virginia, and Boston, Massachusetts. But, a little known fact is that part of George Washington's army is buried near the Ephrata Cloisters in Ephrata, Pennsylvania, and the spirits of '76 aren't always at rest.

During the Revolutionary War, around the time of the battle of Brandywine, at least 200 wounded soldiers were sent to the Ephrata Cloister. It was used as a hospital because of the advanced medical talents of the community.

It's not known if George Washington ever visited his troops there, but he might have. The brothers and sisters of the cloister

The ghosts of Revolutionary War soldiers have been spotted guarding their memorial.

did their very best to heal the wounded soldiers, but some of them did die from their wounds and were buried in what is now known as Mt. Zion Cemetery—next to the Ephrata High School is a football field which is appropriately called Memorial Field.

There is a tall, black monolithic monument surrounded by four small revolutionary war cannons and American flags.

Rumor has it that, on certain nights, the spirits of these fallen soldiers can be seen standing guard over the mass grave of their remains.

To get to the Ephrata Cloister and the Mt. Zion Cemetery from Hershey, go southeast on Park Avenue/PA 743 towards West Chocolate Avenue/US-422, then turn left onto West Chocolate Avenue/US-422 east/PA 743 south. Turn right onto Cocoa Avenue/PA 743, then turn left onto West Governor Road/US 322 east towards Ephrata. The Ephrata Cloisters are located at 632 West Main Street.

The Haunted Mountain Springs Hotel

Although the main buildings no longer exist at the Mountain Springs Hotel, it was the premier vacation destination for the wealthy and famous during the early 1800s. The hotel has had a varied and interesting history from its early days as a health resort to its less than glory days as an abandoned eyesore, looking like the northern version of Disney's Haunted Mansion, and with good cause. If any building deserves to be haunted in Ephrata, this is the one.

The site of the hotel was at the corner of Main Street and Spring Gardens Street. It encompassed an entire city block. The shell of its former self, the crumbling building sat unoccupied by the living for decades until the year 2004, when it was purchased by the Hampton Inn—who tore most of it down,

The old Mountain Springs Hotel, Circa. 2004. Everything from séances to satanic rituals have happened behind these walls.

except for a small section of the original building. They built a Hampton Inn and an Applebee's on the site.

Back in the 1800s, people would travel great distances from Philadelphia and New York just to sample the healing waters and take in the view of the countryside at Mountain Springs. It was said that if you looked out from the observation tower you could actually see as far as Maryland, three states away. It was the destination spot of its time and Milton and Kitty Hershey were probably frequent guests because of Kitty's illness.

Alas, the good times were not to last. Eventually, the hotel fell out of fashion and was sold to the city and became the first Ephrata Hospital for the treatment of mental patients.

Then in 1949, it was sold to a spiritualist group known as the Utopias and they renamed it Camp Silver Bell, after their

Indian spirit guide. It was during this time that the rumors about the haunting of the hotel started circulating. The Utopias, a precursor to the modern-day new age movement held regular séances and hosted spirit materializations.

Spiritualism was a very popular religious and social movement that started back in the mid 1800s. Many intelligent and educated people, such as Abraham Lincoln, Thomas Edison, and Sir Arthur Conan Doyle, the author who created Sherlock Holmes, were all very actively involved in spiritualism. So it was not a fringe cult only practiced by a few crackpots. There is a community of spiritualists in New York State called Lilly dale and you can't even live there unless you're a certified medium.

A few years later, the golden age of mediums and spiritualists died out and the Camp was closed down. This is when people started to call the old hotel "The Spooks." The old building, was reputed to still echo with eerie sounds, cold spots, and the sightings of shadowy figures still roaming its deserted and moldy hallways.

The local ghost hunting groups had tried to gain access to the building to do a full scale investigation, but unfortunately, the owners were unwilling to let anyone inside due to the advanced deterioration of the building—they didn't want the liability of someone getting injured in the process.

That hasn't stopped vagrants and cult groups from invading the property over the years, though. According to one eyewitness, there was once a room on the lower level in the basement that was used by a Satanic cult and had a pentagram inscribed on the floor and mirrors scattered around the room—although there is no way to verify this now, as the person who saw this was trespassing on the property and remains anonymous.

I visited the property a year before it was demolished, and although I would've liked to, I was not there to do any ghosts

Opposite page:
Can you see the ghostly figure in the second window from the left?

hunting. I merely wanted to get some black and white photos of the building before it was torn down in order to do a painting of the building.

I walked around the block this clear sunny day, wanting to get pictures from every angle. I walked up to the front of the main building and snapped off a half a dozen pictures. Since they were for a painting and I could adjust the lighting later, I wasn't very particular about getting the correct lighting. As I walked across the front lawn, I looked at all the broken windows and the dark recesses of the upstairs balconies.

It was a perfect day for picture taking, not too sunny and not very cloudy. I used a whole roll of black and white film. It wasn't until I developed them that I got a surprise. I always like to scan my pictures and put digital copies on my computer. After I first had them developed, I had a few of the whole front view of the building and wanted to enlarge them for framing. It was then that I noticed the odd shadow in one of the windows in the part of the building that faces Main Street. I focused in on the upper floor windows.

There it was, the holy grail of ghost hunting—the distinct shadow of a figure wearing a baseball cap, and in the other window was another shadow figure.

While I was taking the pictures, I also noticed that on the same building, at the corner, one of the shutters on the first floor window slowly opened and closed in front. At first, I didn't take notice; then I realized there was absolutely no breeze blowing that day. And none of the other shutters were moving at all.

Unfortunately, all the remains of the building that once dominated the countryside is the small building that is used as the manager's home for the Hampton Inn.

From Hershey, go southeast on Park Avenue/PA 743 towards West Chocolate Avenue/US-422, then turn left onto West Chocolate Avenue/US-422 east/PA 743 south. Turn right onto Cocoa Avenue/PA 743, then turn left onto West Governor Road/US 322 east towards Ephrata.

The Ghostly Twin of the Old Lincoln Farmhouse

When you live in a century-old building, you get used to the sounds that go with it. Most of the time, they are just normal mundane sounds of the house settling, but then there are other times when they can't be explained by normal means.

Ten years ago, in the early 1990s, a man by the name of Jack related this story to me. He had just moved into an apartment building on the outskirts of Ephrata borough in a town called Lincoln. Lincoln was one of the oldest settlements in the borough of Ephrata.

The building Jack moved into was an old stone farmhouse once owned by a local farming family, not the Abraham Lincoln family, as one might think since it was called the old Lincoln Farmhouse. Originally, the town was known as New Ephrata, but after the assassination of Abraham Lincoln in 1865, it was changed to the name of Lincoln in his honor.

Anyway, Jack moved into the building that was once the main farmhouse of the family that owned the land. The bottom floor consisted of the offices of the travel company called Elite Coach. But upstairs, there was a set of apartments on each side of the building right across from each other. You cannot access the apartments directly. You had to walk up the central staircase and one apartment was on the left and the other was on the right. Jack rented the apartment on the right, and at the time he moved in, he was the only resident. The left apartment was vacant.

Once in, Jack decided that he wanted to repaint the apartment because he didn't like the paint job the previous tenant had given it—he wanted one more suited to his own taste. The apartment was very nicely designed. There was a large bedroom at the back, away from the noise of the traffic on Route 322. The walls were solid stone and the windows, eight in all, had sound muffled glass that made the apartment very quiet when it came to outside noise. This would play a factor in Jack's encounter of the paranormal kind.

The old Lincoln Farmhouse. An untimely death contributes to the haunting of this old building in Lincoln, Ephrata Borough.

The haunted stairway.

Jack quickly settled in, and felt immediately at home. The only strange thing he noticed were sounds coming from the upstairs attic. There was only one access door to the attic for the whole building and this was through his hallway closet across from his kitchen.

When Jack first moved to the apartment, he would swear you could hear the sound of someone up upstairs or someone's pacing back and forth across the attic floor all night long every night. He chalked it up to the sounds of an old house—that is until later when he would have guests over. They also heard the sounds and he had to assure them that nobody was upstairs. After awhile, Jack didn't even notice the sounds anymore; it was only when a visitor came to his apartment that the sounds would be mentioned.

Six months after Jack moved in, the other apartment was rented by man named Frank. Jack met Frank the day he was moving in. He was a big guy at least six feet tall and husky. After some small talk, Jack and Frank had a beer. They both worked a lot of hours and really didn't take much notice of each other over the months that they both had lived next door to each other.

Jack was very busy working a full time job at a company in Honeybrook, Pennsylvania, and he also worked for the newly-opened Walmart part time in the evenings several nights a week.

Frank worked for company in Ephrata called Science Press, a large offset printing company and usually worked a lot of overtime. Both kept to themselves, not because they were unfriendly, but becausethey each had very busy schedules that didn't give them much time to socialize. Jack usually saw Frank on his way to work or coming back from the grocery store and they'd greet one another, making small talk, but usually nothing beyond that. Jack had no idea where Frank was from or anything else about him, and the same went for Frank about Jack. Jack never volunteered much about himself or his personal life, either.

One thing Jack did notice from the very beginning was that when Frank moved into the apartment, he could always tell when he was coming home from work, usually late at night. Frank wore heavy work boots and the acoustics of the stairway left no doubt as to who was coming up the stairs.

A year went by, and one night, a week from Halloween, the unexpected happened. Jack had just gotten home around 11pm from his part time job at the photo lab at Walmart. Frank's truck wasn't parked in the lot next to the building and Jack assumed he was working overtime.

Jack usually watched a little television before going to bed. He tried to keep the noise down because, as soundproof as the outside walls were, the inside walls didn't block sound very well, and on some occasions, he'd had to ask Frank to turn his set down and Frank had asked him to do the same. They mutually respected each other's noise restrictions and after certain hours kept the noise down.

About an hour later, Jack says he heard the familiar heavy tread of Frank's boots approach the stairs go up, and could hear the jingling of his house keys as Frank opened his apartment door. It was something Jack had heard at least thousand times before and didn't give it much thought. He reflexively turned the sound down on the TV and could hear Frank walk around in the next apartment, to lie down half an hour later, then the noise settled. Jack decided to hit the sack for the night as well.

The next morning, Saturday, Jack was heading out around 8am to go to the gym for his daily workout when he encountered Frank moving furniture down the stairs. It looked like he was moving out. Jack said hi and asked him if he was moving? An older man joined Frank who looked very similar to him and Jack assumed it was Frank's dad. The older man asked Jack if he lived in the apartment next door; he said yes. Jack then looked at Frank and asked him where he was moving to. He looked at him for a second and then said, "I'm not Frank. I'm his twin brother Tom."

Jack was surprised. He looked exactly like and sounded and dressed just like Frank. Tom and Frank's father went on to explain to Jack that they had just gotten there this morning, a few at hours ago around 6am.

Then they dropped the bombshell. Frank's dad went on to explain that they had come up that morning to collect Frank's belongings and take them back to Wilmington, Delaware. Tragically, Frank was struck and killed by a truck the day before while crossing a busy street in his hometown of Wilmington. Jack did not know what to say. He conveyed his condolences but, he had to ask again, when did Frank die?

His father wanted to know why Jack didn't believe him. It was then that Jack told them that he thought he'd heard Frank moving around in his apartment late last night. Frank's father grew concerned and said no one should have been there at that time of night. He said he only called the landlord that morning to get the key, so even he wouldn't have known about Frank's death. Jack wondered then who had he heard? He was sure it sounded it exactly like Frank.

Jack continued on his way to the gym after again expressing sympathy to Frank's brother and father. Still, it bothered him about the night before. By the time Jack finished his workout and had finished his errands, Frank's father and brother had left the property.

Jack felt bad for them, but was still bothered by the sound he had heard the night before. He had almost convinced himself that what he had heard was noise from the travel office downstairs and someone was working late. Except that he remembered that all the lights were off downstairs and no cars were parked in the lot. His suspicions that the sounds he'd heard the night before weren't of mundane origin and they were confirmed that same night.

Jack was watching a special on TV about Halloween parades in New York City. He heard the same familiar heavy footsteps clog up the stairway and heard the jingle of keys in the lock of the apartment next door. By the time he got to the hall and open the door, he looked out to an empty staircase. A tingling sensation came over him and he closed and locked his door. What had just happened? He opened the door again and looked; still no one was there.

Jack looked out his window to see if there were any other cars besides his own in the lot—there weren't. It took Jack several hours to get to sleep that night. He kept hearing noises of movement coming from the other apartment—an apartment that he knew was empty, at least of any living presence. He had a feeling he knew what was going on but he needed more proof to confirm his suspicions.

After working the next day, he paid a visit to very good friends of his. Tim and Susan had rented a farmhouse south of town and found it to be haunted. He wanted to talk to them before he jumped to any conclusions about his own situation.

They listened to Jack's story and they agreed that it did sound like Frank's spirit wasn't at rest. Jack was always interested in local ghost tales, but he never expected to be part of one. Another night went by, and at the same time that night, Jack heard the familiar footsteps on the stairs and the jingle of keys. He decided to take matters into his own hands. Frank's spirit kept repeating the same action so Jack was sure that Frank was unaware that he was a ghost. He decided that the next night he would confront the spirit head on and help him if he could.

Jack read that if you talk to a spirit directly and explain their situation to them, they will sometimes be put to rest and this would allow them to move on. In fact, the next night was October 31, and Jack also learned that that was the best time to make contacts with earthbound spirits.

Jack prepared a speech to say to Frank's spirit and had lit several candles around the room. Hoping that what he was about to do would end the spirit's wandering. At exactly the same time as the other nights, the sound of heavy footsteps plodded up the stairs. As soon as Jack heard them he steeled himself and stepped out into the landing facing the stairway and holding a candle. He wasn't sure what he was going to face. The candle flickered in the landing but Jack saw no one.

The stairs were chilly but it could have been because of the cold October air. He cleared his throat and tried to keep his voice steady.

"Frank," he boldly said, " I know you're confused right now, but you've got to listen to me. There's something you've got to know. I know it's going to be hard to accept, but you were hit by a truck last week and died on the spot. Your dad and brother, Tom, were here and took all your belongings with them back home. You don't belong here anymore. You don't need to be here. You need to move on. I'm sorry."

Jack blew out the candle and went back into his apartment. According to Jack, he still continued to hear the footsteps on the stairs for a few weeks; then they seemed to get fainter and fainter as time went by.

A few months later, Frank's apartment was rented out to someone else and they never mentioned anything about strange noises there. Jack moved out a few years later himself, satisfied that he had done his best to help Frank's restless spirit.

The old Lincoln Farmhouse is the Home Office of Elite Coach, but should you want to visit the site from Hershey, go southeast on Park Avenue/PA 743 towards West Chocolate Avenue/US-422, then turn left onto West Chocolate Avenue/ US-422 east/PA 743 south. Turn right onto Cocoa Avenue/ PA 743, then turn left onto West Governor Rd./US 322 east towards Ephrata.

The Ghostly Swimmer

Mike (not his real name), related this story to me. About ten years ago, he joined the Ephrata REC Center. Mike had just moved to the area and found the REC Center's hours and location suited his needs for working out at the gym perfectly.

Mike liked to work out very early in the morning before starting his workday. The Ephrata REC Center was a facility that catered to the community in a variety of ways. It had a weight room, a cardio room, an aerobics room, and a large gymnasium. For entertainment, they had a game room complete with Ping-Pong tables, pool tables, and a large-screen TV. The gym was

Does a ghostly swimmer still do laps in the pool at the Ephrata REC Center

used for local basketball games and volleyball tournaments, craft shows, and other shows were also held there. Additionally, there was a babysitting service and various classes for the community were held in several small classrooms.

One of the largest draws for people to the REC center was its Olympic-size swimming pool. All the local schools used the pool for their swim meets. The pool was also open to the public most days of the week. Lanes were roped off that were used exclusively for lap swimmers.

Mike usually arrived at the Center before it opened in the morning. Day in and day out. He'd show up just before the doors opened at 6am. It seemed that Mike wasn't the only one with that idea. Usually, there would be a crowd of a dozen or so men and women waiting to enter the front doors in the morning. Some of them were working-class people who were trying to get their daily workout exercise in before going to work. Mike was one of them. The others were retired folk. After a few weeks of showing up, Mike got to know some of them.

There was a retired couple, Bill and Shirley, another retired couple, Al and Connie, and a couple of older guy's, Frank and

George. Frank and George were a couple of pistols. They would pass the time waiting for the doors to open by telling really, really bad jokes—the kind of jokes that would make you groan. They would always try to outdo each other to see who could get the worst groan from the rest of the group. You really couldn't miss these guys according to Mike. They were there at the center every day. They never missed a day. They stood out, not only because of their jokes, but because they were really nice guys who regularly took turns holding the doors open for everybody each morning. It was always a bright spot of the day to see them out the front of the REC Center.

George always wore a bright purple ski jacket and carried a bright orange boogie board. Frank was a boisterous heavyset man with a mustache. Several decades earlier, they would have made a headlining vaudeville comedy team. Mike got into the routine of getting to the Center just in time to hear some of their awful jokes, sometimes just getting in after everyone went inside.

One day, on a Monday morning, Mike's alarm failed to wake him and he saw that it was going on 6am. He really needed to get to the gym and workout, as he had been to a party over the weekend and had indulged in too much food and drink. He knew that going to the gym would make him feel better.

Mike was really looking forward to going to the steam room and sweating out some of the toxins he'd imbibed. And besides, if he didn't show up at the gym, he knew everyone would give him a good-natured hard time about slacking off on his workout routine.

Quickly getting dressed and driving the couple blocks from his apartment, he arrived at the parking lot just at 6am—just in time to see the other morning regulars filing in through the front door while Frank held the door.

George looked over at Mike, and grinning, gave him a wave before heading into the lobby of the REC Center. Mike grabbed his bag out of the trunk of his car, quickly slammed it shut, and jogged to the entrance.

Since he was late, he just went directly to the weight room carrying his bag with him. The mood seemed different this morning for some reason. It wasn't something that Mike could actually put his finger on, but different nonetheless. The retired people seemed more subdued than usual. Bill and his wife, Shirley, whispered quietly among themselves. Even Frank seemed down in the dumps.

Mike finished his workout and headed to the locker room looking forward to a soak in the hot tub and a steam in the steam room. While Mike changed into a swim trunks to head out into the swimming pool area to the hot tub in a small alcove off to the main pool, he'd heard snippets of conversation that went like: "He was in good shape..." or "Just goes to show you never know...".

Mike was pretty sure someone had either been injured or had died, but he had no idea who they were talking about. Shrugging it off, he walked out into the pool area. As he walked past the lanes used by George for swimming laps he noticed a sign that normally read: Lap swimming only! It had been replaced with a temporary one that to his surprise read: This lane temporarily closed in honor of George—who passed away last Friday.

Mike, thought to himself, if George died on Friday... How could he have seen him outside this morning? He'd even waved to him! Mike knew he'd seen George that morning, so he decided that maybe he'd talk to Frank to make sure that he had the man's name right. Maybe it was some other George who had died. But deep inside, he really knew the answer.

He took a soak in the hot tub and caught up with Frank in the steam room. Frank confirmed Mike's fear; he wasn't mistaken. George, the George that he knew, had died on Friday. Mike knew then that he had just had seen his first ghost.

Should you want to visit the site, from Hershey go southeast on Park Avenue/PA 743 towards West Chocolate Avenue/US-422, then turn left onto West Chocolate Avenue/US-422 east/ PA 743 south. Turn right onto Cocoa Avenue/PA 743, then turn left onto West Governor Road/US 322 east towards Ephrata. Turn left onto Academy Drive, the REC Center will be on your right.

The Ghost of Apple Street

There is a small, two-story house in Lincoln, Ephrata Borough that dates back to the early nineteenth century. The House has had several owners in its 100-year history. Only the last owner died before they could sell it. She was found dead of natural causes in the living room.

My girlfriend, at the time, purchased the property and I helped her move in. From the very beginning, she felt there was a presence in the house. The house wasn't very big. Just two small bedrooms upstairs. A living room, kitchen downstairs, and a later addition to the house was the bathroom that was attached to the back during the 1950s.

My girlfriend had two cats, one a small black witches cat and the other an all old plump calico. The black cat was a female and the calico a male. Both of the animals always acted skittish in the house. The one cat, the black one, always avoided the living room unless someone was in there with her.

My girlfriend lived there by herself for several years. I moved in for a short time a few years later. During this time, one paranormal occurrence sticks out in my mind. We always kept a dry eraser marking board to leave messages for each other since we had conflicting work schedules. The eraser board was attached to the refrigerator by four magnets that were quite strong. It actually took two hands to pry it off.

One night, about 3am, I was sleeping and woke up to the sound of the black cat screeching and hissing at the top of her lungs and the sound of something ripping and being thrown downstairs in the kitchen. I grabbed my robe and headed down the spiral staircase in the dark to investigate all the noise.

Everything was dark, except for a small beam of light shining in from the street lights outside. I could tell something was different. The black cat was at my heels with her hair sticking straight up and her tail bristling.

When I turned the kitchen light on, I immediately saw what had made the noise. What I couldn't figure out, was why. The sight that greeted me was the dry erase board lying face down on the opposite side of the kitchen, ten feet away from the refrigerator where it normally was attached. But, stuck to the refrigerator were three of the magnets with the backing of the dry erase board still partially attached to them. It looked like someone angrily ripped it off the refrigerator and flung it across the room.

The cats wouldn't enter the room. I should probably mention at this point that I was the only person in the house at the time. In retrospect, I have a feeling why that particular paranormal occurrence happened. Shortly after that incident, my girlfriend and I broke up and I moved out of the house. Was the spirit trying to tell me something? Possibly.

This is a private residence, so no directions are available.

Is That You Poppi?

A little south of Ephrata and east of Hershey is small farmhouse that was once owned by the local Miller back in the 1700s.

Good friends of mine, Ron, Sarah and their two daughters had rented it back in the mid nineties. The property came complete with a large yard with a stream running behind it. What they didn't expect was having an unseen border to interact with them on almost a daily basis.

The farmhouse originally had a large red barn attached to it, and the Mill, which at the time Ron and Sarah rented the property was in ruins, nothing more than a crumbling foundation and a few vine-covered walls that sat alongside the road next to an old covered bridge.

Things were normal at first in the farmhouse. I'd helped them move, and aside from their oldest daughter not liking the house, things were ordinary.

The door to the old farmhouse.

A few weeks later, I was there for dinner and was discussing my ghost hunting group's latest investigation. It was at an old cemetery in Ephrata that was reputed to be haunted. We'd captured a few orbs on the digital camera, but no EVP (electronic voice phenomena). And so we were actually disappointed with much time spent at the investigation and little results to show for it.

I could tell they had something they wanted to tell me and after looking at each other for approval Sarah said, "How would the members of your group feel about another investigation?"

"We are always interested in new locations," I replied. "Where did you have in mind?"

She smiled. "We were hoping you could investigate the farmhouse."

I was surprised. They hadn't mentioned any sort of paranormal activity at the farmhouse before and I'm sorry to say that at that time I was about as sensitive as a brick to the supernatural. I wouldn't have seen a ghost if it had jumped up and said *BOO!*

That was the big joke of our group at the time. Everyone would get a feeling they were being watched, feel cold spots, and even hear disembodied voices. Everyone except me that is. As interested and as enthusiastic as I was about having a paranormal encounters, I can honestly say I'd never had one on any single investigation.

I told Ron and Sarah I'd contact are group (It was comprised of members of the Pennsylvania Ghost Hunters Society) and see how soon we could do an investigation. In the meantime, I asked them to keep track of anything that happened of a paranormal nature around the farm. They agreed and a week later our team assembled to conduct an investigation for them.

There were five of us on the team: Chad handled the thermo scanner during the investigation. Amy, Chad's fiancée, covered taking digital pictures, while I took pictures using a regular film camera loaded with 400 speed film. Two others of our group, friends of Chad, a pair of brothers had an extra digital camera and another thermal scanner and a camcorder.

We started our investigation of the farmhouse by interviewing Ron and Sarah as a group. That way everyone would be in on the same page when it came to the background information.

Ron and Sarah explained to the group that they had just finished moving into the farmhouse when the strange incidences started and have been ongoing ever sense. At first, Ron explained, there was the usual disorganized moving chaos of not being able to find certain items. They originally had thought that one or the other of them had just misplaced boxes. But after talking to each other and then their two daughters everyone in the family realized that some boxes were missing.

All of them searched the house and the garage, but couldn't find what they were missing. Finally they gave up. A few days later Sarah found the boxes as plain as day sitting in the upstairs hallway. A hallway they had all checked days prior.

The oldest daughter, Kate, was not happy and never liked living at the farmhouse. At first they chalked it up to her being a teenager, but after a while, they began to wonder if something else might not be happening.

Sarah only had partial custody of Kate and their youngest daughter, Anne. Sarah was divorced and her daughters spent time at their father's house in Lancaster. Kate's bedroom was a small room upstairs with a homemade built-in water bed next to the wall.

Most teens would have jumped at the chance to have such a great room. Privacy, away from the rest of the family, a loft, and a water bed. But Kate didn't like staying in the room for some reason. She claimed it was incredibly warm all the time, even in the winter when the rest of the house was drafty. She claimed, too, that she never felt like she had any privacy, even though this was probably the most secluded room in the whole farmhouse.

The family pets were also acting strangely, Ron said. The fat, old orange tomcat, Bear, would hiss for no reason in an empty room. And he would always try to get outside of the house. It was simply something he had never done before, being raised as an indoor cat, and until they moved to the farmhouse, he'd never shown any interest in the great outdoors at all. They told us Bear had gotten out once in the past, stepped one foot outside the door, then ran right back in the house. He'd hid for several days after that.

Their dog, a Chihuahua named Wiz, didn't act any less unusual. Wiz, from his perch on the back of the sofa, suddenly would look up, his eyes tracking around the room as if he were watching someone walking around the living room. But everyone was sitting watching TV at the time.

The number one reason they felt the farmhouse was haunted, though, was that all of them had an encounter with what they thought was a female spirit. It would happen any time during the day or night. Ron and Sarah explained that a typical encounter happened like this.

One or two of them would be sitting in the living room, either reading a magazine or watching TV. And the scent of an old-style perfume like lavender water or rosewater would start to heavily permeate the air. Sometimes it would get so stuffy they actually had to open a window, even in the wintertime.

The next thing that would happen is that someone in the room would feel as though someone were standing behind them closely. Ron even mentioned that it felt as though Sarah had come up behind him and put her hand on his shoulder.

After listening to Ron and Sarah, the group decided to split into two teams. Chad and Amy would cover the farmhouse. Myself and the two brothers would investigate the old mill where people had spotted a glowing apparition in amongst the ruins.

Legend had it that the Miller who built the farmhouse and the mill became depressed and hung himself in the old mill and that it was his restless spirit that haunted the grounds around the old mill. We agreed to switch in an hour so. That way, Amy and Chad could investigate the mill while we did our own sweep of the farmhouse.

The investigation went smoothly, although after having thoroughly searched the house, mill, yard, and even the covered bridge, our investigation turned up no orbs, ectoplasm, or smells

Legend has it that the original miller hung himself here and now his spirit haunts the old mill.

Bear, the cat, who has also encountered the female spirit of the farmhouse.

of any kind. Sadly, we had to inform Ron and Sarah that we had no concrete evidence that the farmhouse was haunted.

A few months later, in July, Ron and Sarah were going on a trip out of the country for a week and asked if I'd mind house sitting for them. I'd be the only one in the house except for the cat and dog because the girls were staying at their father's house for the week.

I agreed, and besides, it would give me a chance to conduct my own observation of any paranormal activity going on in the house all that week. They gave me a set of keys to the house and then left for their flight. Even though I was staying overnight at the farmhouse I didn't bring a suitcase because I lived close by and just brought what I needed from my apartment each day.

To tempt fate, I decided to stay in Kate's room each night because that was the most reported area of paranormal activity. I had stayed there before, and Kate hardly ever was around to use it herself. (I found the water bed to be very comfortable to sleep in.)

The first night I stayed at the house, it felt normal. There were sounds, but really they were not that paranormal; it sounded more like pipes rattling or just an old house settling. Nothing out of the ordinary—that was to come later on.

The next day was the 4th of July and I spent it picnicking and visiting my family at a park in Lancaster.

That evening, being a Civil War buff, I decided to start watching the movie *Gettysburg*. The actual battle had taken place during this time of year. I was settled into a lounge chair and was halfway into the movie when I started to smell a lavender sort of musty perfume smell. After a few minutes, it got stronger and it felt like someone had walked up behind me and had leaned over the back of my chair. The overwhelming sensation startled me into knocking my glass of water off the arm of the chair and startled the cat as well. For the first time in all my years of ghost hunting, I actually had a paranormal encounter! I looked around just to make sure no one really was there. No one was. The smell faded away a few minutes later.

I cleaned up my water cup, refilled it, and continued watching the movie for several more hours before going to bed.

About 2am in the morning, awakened out of a sound sleep, I distinctly heard a woman's voice whisper in my ear, "Is that you Poppi?" It was coming from my left side. The side closest to the wall. I even felt a small gust of the air. It felt as if someone was whispering in my ear. The only thing was, I was lying next to the wall and I was alone in the room.

A second time, I heard the voice say "Poppi." I became alert, rolled out of the water bed, stood up in the completely dark room, and promptly tripped over a rocking chair that had been moved from the room's corner to the center of the room—and not by me!

I was disturbed, but not frightened. I went downstairs to the kitchen to get a drink of water and to sort out what had just happened upstairs. I figured whoever was haunting the farmhouse had mistaken me for someone else. Someone named Poppi.

At the time this happened, I had a full beard which had it made me look like the lost member of the band ZZ Top or coincidentally, it could've made me look like an Amish or Mennonite farmer. Perhaps the female spirit was searching for this Poppi and I happened resemble the person. I didn't get much more sleep that night. I could fully understand now why Kate didn't like staying in the room.

The rest of the week went by with no more incidents, but I couldn't shake the feeling that I was being observed every night I stayed in the house.

When Ron and Sarah returned from a Ireland, I told them of my ghostly encounter and they were amazed. The spirit had never spoken to either of them. "Perhaps, she likes single guys, like you," joked Sarah.

Another year went by, and one night Ron called me and said the strangest thing just happened the prior night. He explained what I take to be the best case of Bi-location I've ever heard of. He and Sarah had just gotten home when a co-worker of Sarah's called to thank her and Ron for helping a relative of hers.

There had been a late-night car accident outside of the farmhouse. Sarah said, "You're welcome, but are you sure it was us? I don't remember any accident or helping anyone." She asked Ron if he remembered anything about an accident and he said he didn't either. The woman on the phone, said her relative described them well and the farmhouse in detail and that it had to have been them.

Perplexed, Sarah hung up the phone and looked at Ron and shrugged her shoulders. Could they have been sleepwalking? She didn't think so. Besides, when the accident took place, they weren't even home. They were on a weekend getaway in Gettysburg. So who was there to help the accident victim out? They think it was the resident spirits of the farmhouse.

The only other explanation was that they have an experienced a Bi-location. It's a phenomenon that happens rarely, but has been documented. Sometimes it's called "crisis apparitions." According to Rosemary Ellen Guiley, in her book *The Encyclopedia of Ghosts and Spirits*, Bi-location is an unusual phenomenon in which a person appears to be in two places simultaneously.

It certainly seems like what happened in the case of Ron and Sarah. Eventually, Ron and Sarah moved out of the old farmhouse and bought their own home in Ephrata. But when they moved, it wasn't the end of my association with the haunted farmhouse.

A few years later, I moved to Ephrata and obtained a part time job working in a one-hour photo lab.

While I worked there developing pictures, I had the opportunity to look at hundreds of thousands of photos as they were being developed. One photo in particular I will never forget. It showed two teenage girls standing in front of the farmhouse that Ron and Sarah once rented. They were standing next to a mailbox in front of the wooden split rail fence that bordered the property. What made the picture so unforgettable was what was floating next to them: It was a human-sized black mass that was semi-transparent. You could actually see part of the mailbox through it! You could tell that neither of the girls in the picture had any idea it was there. It was the most amazing ghost picture I'd ever seen.

Unfortunately, the picture had to be shredded. When the customer came to pick up the pictures and they saw what they thought was a bad photo, they decided they didn't want the picture. Photo lab policy stated that if the customer doesn't want to pay for it, the picture must be shredded.

In 2004, I had my last encounter with the haunting of the farmhouse. By this time, all that remained out on the property was the farmhouse. The mill, covered bridge, and the old barn had all been torn down for new development.

I was working as a walking ghost tour guide in Strasburg, Pennsylvania, and one of the stories that the owner of the walking tour wanted us to relate to our tour group was about a haunted mill and farmhouse. It turned out to be the same farmhouse that Ron and Sarah had rented all those years ago. It was amazing to me how far the story of the farmhouse had traveled over the years, only to come back to me through a third party.

I'd like to be able to give you directions, but this is a private residence.

According to four different psychics, more than one spirit haunts the Inn 422.

Chapter 8
Lebanon County Ghosts

Inn 422

What do President James Buchanan, four psychics from Washington State, and the Hershey Trolley Company all have in common? A connection to the property known today as Inn 422.

Tucked back from the highway and surrounded by car dealerships and strip malls sits Inn 422. Closely guarded by a small a contingent of Victorian-style lampposts and weeping willow trees, the Inn 422 looks very much a out of place in the modern era. When the current owners of the Inn bought it in 1995, little did they know that along with the property, they were getting a very special permanent resident.

The estate was in shambles when enterprising couple Scott and Crystal Aungst first acquired the property. Their goal was to restore the property to its original colonial grandeur and turn it into a first-class restaurant and a bed and breakfast.

Almost immediately the spirits made their presence known in small ways to them. The house has a long and varied history. Some of it quite tragic. Especially in the case, of young Miss Anne Coleman.

The original home consists of the front part of the Inn's foundation, built by Robert and Anne Coleman to be a graduation gift for their daughter, also named Anne. She had just graduated from Dickinson College in Carlisle, Pennsylvania. The Coleman's had a large prosperous family, nine sons and five daughters. They were hardworking, sharp witted, and very wealthy. In fact, they were one of the wealthiest families in the nation turn of the eighteenth century. Anne Coleman, after her graduation, returned to Lebanon and started her law practice on the current site of the Lebanon County Historical Society.

So, what could possibly cause such heartbreak that Anne Coleman remains in spirit at the inn? The answer: Enter one James Buchanan, future president of the United States of America. Anne Coleman fell in love with young James Buchanan and thereby sealed her fate.

Unfortunately for Anne, her father was acquainted with James Buchanan from his days at Dickinson College. Anne's father, Robert Colman was a trustee of the college and had previously expelled the young lawyer-to-be for disciplinary action. He later readmitted him and Buchanan was able to graduate. To make the situation worse was his parentage. In those days, who your family was, was just as important as who you were. James was from a small town called Stony Batter near Mercersburg, Pennsylvania. His family had no established roots in the newly-formed United States, and had recently emigrated from Northern Ireland. So in Robert Coleman's eyes, he was not an acceptable choice as a suitor for his daughter, Anne.

In those days, weddings were prearranged among well-to-do families of proper social standing. While Anne built her law practice, James courted her and was a frequent visitor at the Coleman Mansion. He had also set up law practices in Lebanon and in Lancaster Counties. Anne and James traveled in the same social and business circles which also drew them closer together. Anne had her practice in Lebanon and James Buchanan was the assistant prosecutor for Lebanon County, and in the early 1813s, became the first member of the Lebanon Bar Association. By today's standards theirs was a perfect match, but at that time, any kind of relationship, let alone romance, would have been scandalous to the community and a personal outrage for the Coleman family.

They knew their romance was dangerous, but despite that, they became engaged, further outraging the Coleman family.

Robert Colman took matters into his own hands. In those days, he had the legal right to break off their engagement. As a result of his interference, Anne and her father had an emotional confrontation that ended in tragedy. Heartbroken over the actions of her father, Anne Coleman, on December 19, 1819, committed suicide while visiting her sister and uncle in Philadelphia. Overcome with grief or depression to her lost fiancée, James Buchanan, she committed suicide by an overdose of laudanum.

Another version of the story claims that the reason she committed suicide is that she had gotten word that James was being unfaithful and that he had paid a visit to a former lover. This was a case of mistaken intentions. James had been merely visiting a client whose wife had happened to have a previous history with Buchanan before her marriage. James Buchanan tried to explain his actions to her, but Anne's family purposely kept the information from her, hoping to finally end her relationship with Buchanan for once and for all.

Perhaps Anne's spirit has located to the place where she was happiest while she was alive. The place where her and James Buchanan spent their brief time together. Her home in Lebanon. Which is now the Inn 422.

Scott Aungst and his wife, Crystal, are the current owners of Inn 422. After thirty-seven years in the restaurant and hospitality business, the Aungsts decided to purchase the property in the spring of 1995, and to turn it into a Victorian bed and breakfast. They have lovingly and painstakingly renovated the property into the Victorian splendor that is today Inn 422.

On the day that I visited the inn, Scott and the housekeeper, Janice, were kind enough to relate some incidents that have occurred over the years at the inn. Scott gave me a tour of the building and showed me some of the unique features of the colonial-era mansion.

The kitchen has been made into a modern commercial kitchen, with many of the original features. There are several rooms for dining on the first floor. And if you ascend a beautiful wood and spiral staircase to the second floor, there are the guest rooms. Including room 202, where Anne Colman makes her presence known in various ways.

Anne is also not the only ghost haunting the establishment. At least according to four visiting psychics from Washington State who claim that there is at least one other ghost haunting the building. There is a ghost of a little boy wearing knickers and short pants in the style of the 1800s. Who this little boy is, or was, is a complete mystery.

According to Scott, not long after the inn opened its doors to the public, he and his wife received a very strange long distance phone call. A woman representing a group of four psychics traveling to Lebanon to help the local law enforcement agencies, locating missing bodies or missing persons he wasn't sure, called to arrange lodging for herself and her traveling companions. She further went on to explain that all of her group were somehow on the psychic level being drawn to stay at the property. Scott, very surprised, took their reservation to stay for the week.

Usually guests only stay for the weekend, but he and his staff made an exception in their case. Scott also mentioned that despite the fact that they were nationally-known psychics and respected among many law enforcement and Federal government groups for the abilities they possessed, the women were not of the capes, black cats, and crystal balls types of people. In fact, they looked perfectly normal, one being a schoolteacher and another a former nurse.

When the four women arrived, they immediately sensed spiritual activity at the inn. They were given a tour of the inn, and as they walked about the century-old mansion, they were drawn to the second floor, up the wooden spiral staircase. All of them were surprised to be drawn to the same room. Room number 202. This was the room Anne most frequently manifested her activities. The next area they were pulled towards was the old parlor section of the house. It was there that they encountered the little boy's spirit.

Regardless of what ghosts may inhabit the inn, the four psychics were sure of one thing. The spirits weren't harmful, but more of a prankish nature and that no one should feel intimidated or threatened by them. Scott was told by the women that the spirits were pleased with the way they had tried to keep the inn looking as much as the original dwelling from colonial times.

After telling me this, Scott directed me to Janice Phillips, the housekeeper, who has been working for them since they purchased the inn. Janice, in her twelve years of working at Inn 422, has had her share of the unexplained encounters with the spirits of the inn. One of the first encounters Janice had with the unseen guests occurred upstairs in the most haunted room of the inn, room 202.

She explained: "Just like any other day, I was changing the sheets on the queen-sized bed. And as I tried to pull the sheet neatly across the bed and tuck the sides in, there was a large, human-sized air pocket smack in the center of the bed. I tried to push it down, but even after a few minutes, it still wouldn't flatten out." In frustration, she called out, "Okay! Anne, you can have the bed!" And she then moved on to clean the next room.

A short while later, she went back to room 202, which had remained unfinished, and to her surprise, the bed sheet was perfectly flat and tucked in on the bed. She was the only housekeeper upstairs that day and still has no explanation except that Anne's spirit wanted the bed at that time.

Janice also told me there were times when she would walk through the upstairs hallway and a gust of cold air would hit her in the face and then disappear.

Janice also pointed out to me a large mirror at the top of the wooden spiral staircase across from a sign that reads: Guests of the inn of only beyond this point. In the surface of the mirror, the reflection a smiling female has been noticed out of the corner of not only Janice's eyes but of several guests at the inn as well.

Staff members are not the only ones who have noticed spiritual activity at the inn. Guests have also felt the prankish spirits' attention. One of the frequent guests was a handicapped man

The spirit of Ann Coleman has been seen several times in this mirror.

One of Ann's favorite rooms.

with an artificial leg; he told the owners several times that he had to get up in the morning and hop across the room on one leg to retrieve his other leg because someone or something had moved it from his bedside in the middle of the night while he was sleeping—and I might mention that he was sleeping alone in the room!

Janice was cleaning the downstairs dining room when I had finished my photo tour of the upstairs. She called me over and held her up cleaning bucket, "Once," she said, "I was carrying this bucket down the hall upstairs and it was full of warm water. As I walked, someone tipped the bucket and spilled all the water all over the floor. But there was no one else there."

When I looked at the bucket, it was just a normal plastic bucket, so were the spirits at it again? Janice certainly thought so.

Seems as though the spirits like to decorate the inn at times, as Scott's wife's daughter had displayed some pillows on one of the couches and left the room for a few seconds. When she stepped back in the room, the pillows had moved and no one—and let me clarify this—*no one* had been around to move them. Even with all the ghostly activity at the inn, Scott and Crystal, Janice, and all the other staff feel relaxed and welcome there and so will you, if you come to visit.

One last note, while I am a certified photographer, I encountered a problem taking pictures at the inn and so have other people. My first set of pictures taken on my Sony digital camera, which was working a few minutes earlier outside just fine, would take only blurry fuzzy out-of-focus pictures inside the building. I Checked all the settings to make sure I hadn't inadvertently changed something. But no, all the settings were set correctly. All of my first pictures were blurry. And then I thought, maybe the spirits are messing with my camera. I hit upon an idea to ask permission of Anne and any other spirits in the house to take pictures. Strangely enough. Once I voiced my request out loud, my camera started working perfectly and each picture came out crystal clear.

So, if you're ever in the area of Lebanon Pennsylvania, and you're hungry for some food and spirits, stop at Inn 422 and treat yourself some award winning food, and say "Hi" to Anne and her little friend. You might even get a hello back.

To get the Inn 422, from Hershey take 422 east towards Lebanon. The Inn 422 will be on your right.

The Rexmont Inn

Off of the main highway of Route 322 sits the sleepy little town of Rexmont, Pennsylvania. (Rexmont is most well known for its haunted location, the Cornwall Furnace—which we will talk about in the next chapter.)

Located at 299 Rexmont Road, across from the Rexmont Fire Company, is a corner building that is immense for such a small town. Granted, there's no sign proclaiming that this is the Rexmont Inn, and if I hadn't been looking for it, I probably would never have found it. From the outside of the building, I would never guess that this small mansion was a bed and breakfast. It looks more like an old mansion that has been converted into apartments. After going around the corner, I looked up to the side of the brick building and noticed a black metal object that spelled out the word REX in bold capital letters.

The outside of the Rexmont Inn, is subdued, but then the outside it isn't the interesting part of the building. It's what, or should I say *who*, is inside that really matters to us.

According to several different eye witnesses, the Susan Amanda room, named after Cyrus' niece who lived with him, is haunted.

The female half of a couple staying in the room reported that she had felt someone sit down behind her on the bed. She thought it was her husband but, when she turned around see who it was, she saw a vaporous figure stand up and walk to front of the bed and then stand just stand there. Meanwhile, she realized that her husband was asleep on the other side of the bed and hadn't moved. Although she couldn't make out the shape of the figure, she wasn't scared, just confused. And then the figure disappeared.

The Rexmont Inn, where the haunting is a drag—literally!

This isn't the first guest to experience this apparition. In fact, there are several other incidents that have happened at the nineteenth century inn.

Ninety years after the death of Cyrus Rex, the first owner and builder of the house and the founder of the town of Rexmont, the large front tower was torn down, and in the meantime, the building was starting to become run down from neglect.

When the owners, George and Janet Ruby, bought the crumbling Victorian mansion, they realized a lot of work would be needed to turn the property into their dream of an elegant inn. During the renovation of the building, the construction contractors, Georgia and Janet Ruby, and even Janet's father, all had encounters with whatever, or whoever, still resided in the old mansion.

It's not unusual, for spirits and hauntings to become more active when renovating a building. The workers often told Janet that they had the feeling someone was watching them as they worked alone.

According to some parapsychologists, there's a theory that spirit energy is imprinted in all the houses via electromagnetic storage—much like how all the reel to reel and cassette tape and video tape record sounds and pictures. When something traumatic has happened in a building, the theory is that we, as living beings, give off an energy field and this energy field imprints itself onto rust in the building, whether it be nails or metal pipes or some other kind of rust. Certain people have a way of picking up on this energy imprint. Those people are psychic or just lucky enough to be in the area when the conditions are right for the playback of the energy. It's possible the workers were picking up on this energy because they had disturbed the rust and dispersed the energy into the surrounding area. While they were working, the activity and feeling of being watched might have increased because the rust had lain dormant for so long.

Over an undetermined period of time the rust and energy will probably settle down and the energy will subside making the area less actively haunted, unless for some reason the released energy finds another source to imprint or that is disturbed on a more regular basis.

On the other hand, maybe it was simply Cyrus Rex's or Susan Amanda's spirit overlooking their handiwork in restoring their home.

Janet Ruby laughingly dismissed the workers' concerns, that is until the night before the public opening of the Inn. She was up in the Cyrus Rex room and then felt the same being watched feeling as the workers.

She also saw a few weeks later what looked like two bright iridescent columns of smoke in the second floor hall around the area where the door to the tower used to exist. A psychic who visited the Inn claimed that the energy source from the now demolished tower was still present.Several other incidents have occurred over the years at the inn.

Janet's father, who was living in the inn for a while, noticed several times that he felt as if someone had brushed past him and heard what sounded to him like the rustle of a woman's gown behind him as he walked.

During the days when no guests had been staying at the inn, Janet and her father have both heard the sound of footsteps and doors slamming upstairs though no one had been there. They have also spotted lights turning on and off when no one's been anywhere near them.

Janet's husband, George, is of a more skeptical opinion when it comes to whether the inn is haunted or not, but there have been some incidences that make him scratch his head in wonder. George moved a grandfather clock that had been in his family for generations, since the 1700s, and has always worked perfectly until he moved it into the sitting room at the Rexmont Inn. Now it stops inexplicably and for no reason or resets the time on its own choosing. Other clocks in the house, such as the library clock and a brand newly-bought clock for the kitchen also act erraticly, resetting themselves at random or ringing too many times.

But who is the spirit, or spirits, that haunt the inn? There are several theories. One theory is that it's the ghost of Cyrus Rex himself looking over the property. Several people have witnessed what looks to be a indistinct figure in a flowing gown of the 1800s, but if this is the case, could it be Mr. Rex?

Cyrus Rex was a very private person, as I mentioned earlier; he was a confirmed bachelor, which in the day, meant that he was gay. Cyrus was well liked in town and it was no secret to the locals that he was what we call today a crossdresser. He liked to wear women's clothes, so it's not outside the realm of possibility that the spirit of Cyrus Rex could being enjoying one of his favorite pastimes as an apparition. Then again, the spirit could be that of his niece, Susan Amanda, as her old bedroom is one of the hot spots of paranormal activity in the building.

If you ever find yourself staying at the Rexmont Inn, and happen to catch a glimpse of someone wearing a ruffled dress or hear the rustling of petticoats follow you down the hall to your room, it just might be Cyrus himself having a bit of drag fun in the afterlife.

To get to the Rexmont Inn from Hershey, go towards West Chocolate Avenue/US 422, turn onto Cocoa Avenue/743 south, then turn left onto Route 322 east. Turn left onto West Main Street/PA 419, then turn left onto Schaeffer Road. Turn right onto Store Lane, then turn left onto Rexmont Road. The Rexmont Inn will be on your left.

Moonshine Church

Located in Indiantown Gap, in Lebanon County, about five miles away from the town of Hershey is a little church called Moonshine and a cemetery with the same name.

The land and the church were donated by Henry Moonshine (1768 to 1836) for the use of the Lebanon community. The original log cabin church burned down in the 1960s and the church that sits on the property was built in 1961.

The Moonshine Church. Don't shut off your car engine at night here—it just might not start up again.

The Moonshine Church graveyard, where Joseph Raber's spirit has been contacted.

There are several ghost stories surrounding this tiny red and white church. Tales of murder, and tragedy are closely connected with the small structure. The most famous of these tales concerns the murder of Joseph Raber and his murderers, the so-called "Blue-Eyed Six."

In 1876, a gang of six men, all of whom had blue eyes, named: Israel Brandt, Josiah Hummel, Charles Drews, Franklin Stichler, Henry F. Wise, and George Zechman, were arrested for the murder of Joseph Raber.

According to the trial records, the six men took out a life insurance policy on Joseph Raber, who was a local laborer living in a small home, not more than a shack, with his common law wife.

The six men were not related to Raber, but in those days, they didn't need to be related—all that was required was that they keep up the payments on the policy. If they did so, then when Raber died, they would collect either $8,000 or $10,000—no one knows for sure. This was all perfectly legal in those days.

The plot thickens at this point. The six men decided to hasten Mr. Raber's death by drowning him in Indiantown Gap Creek. The men surrounded him and pushed him into the creek and then two of them held him helplessly under the water until he died.

All of this was going according to plan, but they, unfortunately, voiced their plans a little too loudly at a local tavern and were overheard planning the evil deed. All of the six men were arrested for Raber's murder. After a hotly publicized trial, all but one of them (George Zechman) were found guilty and were hanged at the corner of Eighth and Chestnut Streets in the city of Lebanon. As a side note, George Zechman died less than a year later. Perhaps the curse of the blue-eyed six caught up with him after all.

Joseph Raber's body was buried in the Moonshine Cemetery. All of the Blue-Eyed Six bodies were buried at their various homesteads or elsewhere, other than Moonshine, although rumors persist that at least one or more of them were secretly buried in the Moonshine Cemetery at a later date.

The most persistent rumors about Moonshine Church claim that if you stop your car near the church, you'll see either a set of glowing blue eyes in the cemetery or along the road. Could this be the ghost of the unjustly killed Joseph Raber? Some people believe it's the spirits of the Blue-Eyed Six, although why would the murderers be hanging about the graveyard where the victim was buried is unclear. More likely, it's the ghost of Joseph Raber who also had blue eyes.

Joseph Raber and his murderers aren't the only haunts associated with Moonshine Church. An urban legend has it that a young local girl who entered the little church took her fate in her hands by reciting the *Lord's Prayer*, only backwards. Why? We have no idea. She was immediately struck down by lightning and killed instantly. Perhaps this is how the church burnt down in the 1960s. After the church was rebuilt, her spirit has been haunting it ever since.

Another story, not substantiated by any facts that I could find verified in the local papers, was that a woman suffered a nervous breakdown and took her four young children to the church, killing them before committing suicide. This was supposed to have happened in the 1980s.

Perhaps the land had been a sacred Indian burial ground for the local Indian tribes. Eye witnesses have spotted several native American spirits roaming around in the Moonshine Cemetery, and one of the most famous and feared is the spirit known as "red devil." Why he was so feared is unknown. There's even a headless horseman spirit that reputedly haunts the area, along with being spotted in other places in Lebanon County.

With all the paranormal goings on in the area, it was inevitable that ghost hunters would seek out the area. Kelly Weaver and her group in Dauphin County, known as Paraseekers, made contact with the spirit of Joseph Raber during the course of their investigation. The now-deceased laborer was amazed at the amount of attention being paid him, seeing how he was very unimportant while he was alive. Kelly's group also found several other spirits of unknown origin haunting the cemetery and church grounds.

If you decide to visit Moonshine Church be aware that there is a large **No Trespassing** sign painted on the building and that you should be respectful as if you were at any other place of worship. Oh, and one other thing—don't turn off your car engine. The spirits might not let you turn it back on.

The Headless Copter Pilot

Not far from Moonshine Church is a military base called Fort Indiantown Gap. This story comes to me via one of the Misfits of the Hotel Hershey. I was interviewing her about the hotel when she mentioned that her husband, Chet, had been a security guard at the heliport at Fort Indiantown Gap, and had told her of a bizarre and frightening incident that happened to him years ago while he was on guard duty.

Chet was on duty one night at his usual post when, out of the darkness, walked one of the helicopter pilots. The pilot approached him, and as he came into the light, Chet recognized him as one of the regular pilots. The man asked him for a set of locker keys—not an unusual request since Chet was in charge of distributing locker access keys. What *was* strange was that when he looked for the keys, he found that he didn't have them on his list. What was even stranger is that Chet had heard that this particular pilot had been killed in an accident a few days earlier. Thinking that maybe he had made a mistake, he informed the pilot that a mistake had been made and that he didn't have his keys. The pilot looked confused but accepted his explanation and walked away into the darkness. Chet scratched his head and made a mental note to ask somebody about the keys later on that day when his superiors were on duty.

At the end of his shift, Chet went to the main office to ask about the pilot's keys. The answer he got chilled his spine. The pilot asking for his keys had indeed been killed, and in rather nasty accident—he had been decapitated and died instantly. Chet, nerve racked and shaking, went home to get some sleep, although it was hard for him to do so after that revelation.

But the worst was yet to come. Chet, a little nervous but still not convinced that he hadn't just made a mistake in thinking he saw the deceased pilot, had convinced himself by the time that he went back to work that it was all a misunderstanding. A case of mistaken identity on his part.

That night, around the same time as the previous one, Chet was working security again when the same pilot walked up to him and requested his keys again! Only this time, according to Chet, he looked like he was from beyond the grave. Chet described him in these words: pale, cadaverous, and acting strangely. Chet, not knowing what else to do, told him once again that he did not have his keys. Shaken and nervous, he watched the man walk off into the shadows; this time he knew he was not mistaken and had just talked to a dead man.

Give Chet some credit, though! He finished his shift and went home, although he spent most of the time looking over his shoulders for the unexpected apparition to appear again.

The Haunted Hunter

In Lebanon County, not far from Hershey, and right up the road from the Rexmont Inn, is the historic Cornwall iron furnace. The Cornwall furnace has been in existence since it was built by a man named Peter Grubb in 1742.

The site holds the distinction of being the only intact charcoal burning iron blast furnace still in its original location in the western hemisphere. It holds another honor as well: It's got a haunted legend attached to it.

Peter Grubb, who named the furnace Cornwall after the location of his father's birth in Cornwall, United Kingdom. Grubb was born in Delaware and moved to Lebanon county in 1734, where he bought 300 acres of land and built his first furnace. Peter Grubb's furnace operation was a huge success. It w asn't the only furnace in the area, but because of the abundant natural resources of white limestone and magnetite it was able to compete with the other twenty-one blast furnaces and forty forges and other steel mills throughout colonial Pennsylvania.

The haunted Cornwall Furnace. where Iron Baron Peter Grubb sacrificed his sanity and his pack of hunting dogs.

Life working the iron furnace was a tough one. At least for the common workers. The owners, like Grubb, lived in big mansions like medieval barons, while the workers lived in small hovels and worked very hard for long days and very low wages.

Like many of his colonial contemporaries, Iron Baron Peter Grubb had much more leisure time than his workers and supposedly one of his major passions was hunting. Purportedly, the story or urban legend, take your pick, is that Grubb was entertaining high-class friends from Philadelphia around the year 1750.

Grubb was bragging about how fine his hunting dogs were and how they never failed to find game for hunting. His friends were less than impressed with his talk, and Grubb, well known for his temper, was provoked. Determined to show them just how good his dogs were, he suggested on the morrow they go a' hunting and then they'd eat those words. Literally.

The next day dawned and Peter Grubb and his prize pack of over forty hunting dogs were loosed on to the countryside to scare up game. Unfortunately, after several hours, the dogs failed to sniff out any game at all. Not even a rabbit.

Good natured ribbing by his friends only rubbed Peter Grubb the wrong way and he began to drink, and the more he drank, he became angrier and more embarrassed. He began to furiously whip the dogs with his riding crop until their fur coats were covered in bloody lather. Now Grubb's friends grew uneasy. The day that started out as a lark was starting to border on madness.

Enraged beyond rational thought, Grubb drove his dogs past the split in the road that led to the village and their kennels, and straight to the blast furnace. He ordered the workers there to toss the mangy curs into the furnace. The workers fearful of the raving madman fled the scene. Grubb's friends tried to calm him down but to no avail. He grabbed the dogs, one in each hand and flung them into the blazing furnace one by one, till the only dog left was the lead dog, his favorite. Finally, it seemed that merciful sanity might have returned to Grubb. But it was too late. The lead dog, fearing for its life after seeing the rest of the pack sacrificed, leapt to attack Grubb's throat. But Grubb was too quick and grabbed the dog by the scruff of her neck and pitched her into the furnace along with the others.

Shaking their heads in horror, his friends quickly retired, gathered there belongings and returned to Philadelphia—leaving the madman to his own devilish company. It has been said that after that episode, Peter Grubb was never the same sane man he once was. He became extremely depressed (after sobering up) and he realized what he had done. This depression followed him for years.

Grubb contracted a fever that left him bedridden in the last days of his life. Whether it was the high fever or something of the more supernatural nature, Grubb claimed that he was being chased around his room by a fiery spirit dogs, barking flames and glaring at him with a red hot coal eyes. At the height of his sickness, he leapt out of his bed, raced around his room three times all the while yelling, "Good God! Good God! The hounds! The hounds are after me!" And then he collapsed dead on the spot.

The Cornwall furnace became obsolete in the 1880s and the last owner, Robert Habersham Coleman (yes, he was of the same Colemans that owned the mansion that is now the Inn 422), shut down the operation on February 11, 1932.

In 1932, Margaret Coleman Buckingham deeded the furnace and the outbuildings to the state, and since then, they've been restored and are now open for tours to the public.

On nights of the full moon, it's been said you can sometimes see strange lights in the woods surrounding the Cornwall furnace site and people have reported seeing a ghostly figure on horseback believed to be the spirit of Peter Grubb and being surrounded or hounded by his prized hunting dogs.

From Hershey, go towards West Chocolate Avenue/US 422, turn onto Cocoa Avenue/743 south, then turn left onto Route 322 east. Turn left onto West Main Street/PA 419; stay on this road. It will eventually become Boyd Street. Follow the signs to Cornwall Furnace.

Railroad Ghosts of Rausch Gap

The ghost town called Rausch Gap was once the largest coal mining town in the Saint Anthony wilderness area. Boomtowns appeared and flourished for a while and then just as quickly died between the years 1830 and 1910.

Rausch Gap grew up rapidly in 1850, when the Dauphin and Susquehanna Coal Company built a railroad up through the Susquehanna River to the town. Rausch Gap became an important rail center. By 1860, the population had grown to 1,000. Most of them were workers and families of the mines and railroad.

Our sad story concerns a man whose job was to throw the train switch that ran past the mine. Oddly enough, it's not his ghost that haunts the rail line. Seems that the man died. How he died is a mystery. His wife was mourning the loss of her husband and she forgot to throw the train switch which led to a horrible train wreck claiming many lives. The victims of that accident were buried in a mass grave that was unmarked in the woods behind the town cemetery.

In the aftermath of the accident, tempers flared and someone needed to be a scapegoat. The railroad claimed it was the wife's fault for not performing her family duty. The emotions ran high and a mob mentality quickly escalated into talk of lynching her. But that's all it amounted to, talk—not because they wouldn't have gone through with it, but because the woman took the matter into her own hands and threw herself in front of a speeding locomotive. Thus ending her life.

It's her tragic spirit that haunts the woods of what's left of the rail bed where she killed herself. Her spirit walks the fateful area holding a lantern. Perhaps she's looking for her husband or more likely the mass graves of the train wreck victims. In either case, people have reported that the temperature will drop and a depressed feeling permeates the area when her spirit manifest itself.

The town died when the mine closed. After the closing, the railroad was rerouted to the Pine Grove Station and that sounded the final swan song for Rausch Gap. In 1875, there were less than 100 people living in the town. By the year 1883, Philadelphia and Reading Railroad, now the owners of the property, removed and dismantled what buildings were left. All of the living residents of the town had departed by the year 1910, and Rausch Gap was literally a ghost town.

Rausch Gap still has its use today. It's one of the stops along the Appalachian Trail where hikers and campers can stop to rest. Just be careful not to let the ghostly woman spot you. Legend has it that if she sees you, she'll run straight at you—and then through you. If this happens, better take out a large life insurance policy, because you'll be doomed to have an accident that will make it look like you were hit by a train.

Take I-81 to the exit for Lickdale/Lebanon Route 72, turn left onto Fisher Avenue, then turn left onto Route 72 north, pass through the Swatara State Park; the road will become Route 443, take Goldmine Road to the top of Second Mountain and then descend to Stony Valley. Rausch Gap is four miles down the trail.

The Kleinfeltersville Hotel

Imagine living in a building that's so haunted you try to put up a barricade every night to keep the ghosts from bothering you. Heather Hollinger can and does. Heather and her husband own the Kleinfeltersville Hotel and Tavern in Kleinfeltersville, Pennsylvania.

According to local legend as reported by *The Talon*, a Lebanon County newspaper, the hotel was built around 1898. The original owner, his name is unknown, went berserk and murdered his wife and children. He dragged and hid the bodies in a meat locker down in the basement of the hotel.

The restless spirits of the murdered woman and her two children are said to still be haunting the hotel. Outside the hotel, the spirits are said to have accosted patrons who are trying to enter the hotel. Officially, the Lebanon County Historical Society claims there was never a murder that took place there. Be that as it may, Heather, her husband, and patrons believe it's haunted. By who, they're not sure.

The Hollingers have heard the sound of many people moving around in the bar room late at night. Normally that'd be music to their ears. But at the time they heard the sound, the bar was closed for the night.

A group of ghost hunters from Lebanon investigated the old hotel, but aside from getting a large amount of a orbs they haven't found any positive proof of a haunting.

To get to Kleinfeltersville from Hershey, go towards West Chocolate Avenue/US 422, turn onto Cocoa Avenue/743 south, then turn left onto Route 322 east. Turn left onto West Main Street/PA 419, then turn left onto Schaeffer Road, turn onto East Main Street/PA 897, then turn left onto Albright Road.

Haunts of Higher Learning

Eight miles east of Hershey, on over 300 acres of rural farmland, sits the campus of Lebanon Valley College. The college was founded in the mid 1800s. It has twenty-five residence halls that house the 1,770 undergrad and graduate students, and 100 full-time faculty members.

At least three of those halls are haunted. One of those haunted dorms is the Mabel Silver Residence Hall. The hall is for female dorm students only, and evidently, the resident spirit, who not so coincidentally happens to be the halls namesake, Mabel Silver, has taken it upon herself to look over the girls who reside there.

Mabel, it seems, doesn't like men visiting the hall. Her portrait hangs in the lobby of the hall. Men who have visited claimed that her eyes follow them around the lobby. Then again,

One of the many haunted dorms of Lebanon Valley College.

maybe they have something to be guilty about. Her overzealous spirit has also been known to give them the bums rush and shove them out the door.

You can't miss the North College dorm, it's a big white building right in the middle of campus. Students who live there have felt the unnerving experience of being watched and disembodied footsteps have been heard in the halls, not to mention some poltergeist activity involving moving furniture and finding initials carved into different objects. Nobody has ever figured out who the phantom carver really is.

The last spot on our haunted campus tour is the Mary Capp Green Hall. The spirit of a little girl who was killed while playing on the railroad tracks that run by the outside of the dorm has been seen playing in the halls. Hopefully, she's learned her lesson about playing on railroad tracks.

Directions from Hershey, go towards West Chocolate Avenue/US 422, take 422 east to Annville. Turn left onto north White Oak Street/934 north. You will be in the center of the campus.

The Haunted Batdorf Building

The Batdorf Building once hosted a restaurant known as the Olde Annville Inn. The building is known to be at least 300 years old. Built by a man by the name of John Batdorf, it is reputed that his snappy-dressed phantom, complete with a top hat, has been spotted in the old establishment.

Over the years, the Batdorf Building has had several tenants on the third floor. A gun and sporting club called the Pennsylvania Sons of America used it up until 1933. Supposedly, it's not been used since then, and according to the owners, loud parties have been heard on that floor by tenants living in the second floor apartments. Since the organization stopped renting the hall seventy years ago, one can only wonder what spiritual goings on are occurring up there.

The haunted Batdorf Building.

The most active haunting of the Batdorf Building was back in the early 1980s when the Olde Annville Inn occupied the building. Both staff members and the owners had frequent encounters with the spirits of the old establishment. Jenny, a waitress, claims to have seen the spectral figure of a man wearing a top hat. She always saw him standing along the wall off to the side of the dining room watching her perform her duties, but as happens a lot of times, when she'd look directly at him, he'd disappear.

It seems that Jenny wasn't the only one to see the dapper man in the top hat. After years of keeping the secret to herself, Jenny asked her coworkers if they'd ever seen anything strange, and all of them, including the owners, had seen him as well.

Denise and Dale Snyder purchased the Batdorf Building in 1980, and shortly thereafter realized that they'd inherited more than just an old building. The Snyder's weren't frightened by all the paranormal activity, according to Denise Snyder. There's nothing scary at the inn and she claimed that she's never been scared to spend time alone there.

Other people have heard some disembodied sounds of a spoon clinking in a cup, sounding like someone stirring coffee. The sound of a table being dragged across the floor has also been heard.The Snyder's felt that it was an asset to have the inn haunted. "It's nothing scary; we had had fun with it," the Snyder's claimed.

The Batdorf Building no longer hosts the Olde Annville Inn. Part of it is currently empty and available for lease.

To get to the Batdorf Building from Hershey, go towards West Chocolate Avenue/US 422, take 422 east to Annville. The Batdorf Building is in the center of town.

Chapter 9

Haunts nearby Hershey

Haunted Indian Echo Caverns

Three miles west of Hershey, off Route 322, is a fascinating, 44,000,000-year-old series of limestone caves known as Indian Echo Caverns. Originally discovered by the Susquehanna Indians and subsequently named for them, the caverns have a fantastic array of underground wonders. There are stalagmites and stalactites in colorful shapes and even an underground lake. And if the stories are to be believed, there is also a horrifying specter that sometimes makes its presence known.

The cavernous rooms were first used over 300 years ago by the Susquehanna Indians who lived along the Swatara Creek in Dauphin County. They used the caves as a shelter against the sometimes brutal Pennsylvania winters, because the caves maintain a steady fifty-two degree temperature. Although they used the caverns, there was one room they felt was possessed by evil spirits: The Rainbow Room!

Hundreds of years later, several people have reported seeing a malevolent, if not downright horrifying, apparition in the Rainbow Room. It's of an angry glaring native American spirit that menaces them and then brandishes the severed head of an old white-bearded white man. Many people have reported seeing this horrible scene over a dozen times since 1987.

The caverns used to host a Halloween haunted tour, but too many people were being frightened by all of this and they discontinued the tours. Other shadowy forms have also been seen in the Rainbow Room. The Susquehanna Indians felt quite the opposite about the room called the Indian Ballroom, a 110-foot-wide cavern; they thought it was populated by beneficial nature spirits and actually used the cavern for initiation ceremonies. They also felt that the underground lake, Crystal Lake, which is a very calm body of water 125 feet underground, was also inhabited by good spirits. Sadly, the Susquehanna Indians vanished during the 1670s leaving the area uninhabited. Besides the local Indian tribes, the cave has played host to other residents.

During the colonial period, a man known as the Robin Hood of Pennsylvania, David "Robber" Lewis, used Indian Echo Caverns as one of his many hideouts. David Lewis was born in 1790 in Carlisle, Pennsylvania. He made a name for himself as a counterfeiter in New York, but later, he was captured, then escaped and returned to his native land of Pennsylvania. It was then that he started being called the "Robin Hood of Pennsylvania" because he robbed many of the wealthy citizens and tax collectors and then shared his ill-gotten gains with the local less fortunates. Hiding out in several local caves throughout the area, including Indian Echo, he was able to keep one step ahead of the law. Because he was well liked by the local populace, they helped cover his tracks. Lewis' career was short lived, however. He was captured and shot during a robbery in Belle Font, Pennsylvania, and died of gangrene at the age of thirty.

While he was dying in jail, he bragged that he had several caches of money scattered in various caves. Perhaps he buried some of his swag at the Indian Echo Caverns and his spirit is still searching for it, or perhaps he's guarding it, waiting to distribute it to some down-on-his-luck person who needs it. In any event, it's clear that "Robber" Lewis was always quick to share with regular folks, and maybe, just maybe, this spirit still roams the area looking to help someone out.

The parking lot where Elizabeth Wilson's spirit has been seen wandering.

William Wilson and his Sister Elizabeth Wilson

Another famous guest of the Indian Echo Caverns was a hermit named William Wilson, who was so famous that one of the caverns is named after him.

William Wilson, had become a legend of Pennsylvania folklore by the late eighteenth century and early nineteenth century. He is most commonly called the Pennsylvania Hermit after suffering a family tragedy involving his sister, Elizabeth. He went mad and withdrew from normal society, spending years aimlessly wandering across southwestern Pennsylvania. Eventually, he settled down and lived his last nineteen years of his life in one of the cavern rooms of the Indian Echo Caverns. The room where he spent his last years and died in are reportedly called the: Wilson Room.

But, what really happened to William and Elizabeth all those centuries ago that spawned numerous ghost stories across three counties? There have been several versions of what happened. The one most often repeated is thought to be the most accurate and most popular. William Wilson and his sister, Elizabeth, were born and raised in Chester County Pennsylvania—either in the East Bradford or West Bradford Townships. They grew up on a family farm, nothing spectacular, but it gave them a modest means of existence. Conflicting sources indicate that William was born in 1764, and his sister was born in 1766, but other sources claim that Elizabeth was born in 1758, and her Brother William was her younger brother.

The Wilson farm was in support of the British during the Revolutionary War, and as a result of their loyalty to the crown, much of their property was confiscated by the continental forces as punishment for that loyalty. Their mother died when William and Elizabeth we're still young children. Their father then remarried a woman who was not fond of her new stepchildren, and as soon as they were of legal working age, she suggested they be sent away. She urged their father to apprentice them off as soon as possible.

At sixteen, which was normal for his age, William was apprenticed to a man known as Fahnestock, a stonecutter who lived in next county over, in Lancaster, fifty miles from his home. Elizabeth was also shipped out to Philadelphia where she was employed as a worker at the Indian Queen Tavern. Elizabeth, while working at the tavern, met a man who was a frequent patron. They had an affair which ended when the man disappeared and left her pregnant. The owners of the tavern, felt this pregnancy was an embarrassment and sent her back home to her family farm.

In October of that year, she gave birth to twin boys. Elizabeth was evidently still able to contact her lover and the father of her children. Shortly after giving birth to her sons, when she was well enough to travel, she had agreed to meet him in nearby Newtown Square. She was hoping to convince him to marry her and help raise the children.

On her way to the rendezvous, she mysteriously disappeared for several days. Strangely, she reappeared, but the children were nowhere to be found.

Even in those early days of the country, the disappearance of two infant children still caused alarm among the community and a search was made by the local townsfolk. The children's bodies were soon found hidden in the very same woods were Elizabeth had last been seen.

Elizabeth was quickly arrested for their murder. A year later, she was found guilty of murdering her two bastard male children and sentenced to death by hanging on December 7, 1785.

Meanwhile, her brother, William, was unaware of her crimes while working in Lancaster. When word finally reached him, he immediately left his employer and traveled to the Chester County jail where his sister was awaiting her execution.

After a brutal ride, he arrived on December 3rd, only a few days before her scheduled hanging. Elizabeth was shocked to see her brother so close to her execution. William managed to do what no one else was able to. He persuaded Elizabeth to tell him the truth surrounding her children's murders. He assembled a group of officials, including the Judge named Atlee, who had sentenced her at the trial, to witness her confession. Elizabeth claimed that her lover, the father of her children had agreed to meet with her in Newtown Square, but she unexpectedly met him in the wooded area about three miles to the west of town. He then proceeded to kill the children and threatened her life if she ever mentioned his involvement in the murder.

Officials signed that they had witnessed a confession and William took the signed confession to the ruling council of the land on December 6, 1785, just one day before Elizabeth was to be hung. Benjamin Franklin was the president of the council, and at his order, the council ordered the execution to be postponed until January 3, 1786, so that they could deliberate the case further.

Relieved by their decision, William breathed a sigh of relief and promptly set about on a course of action to see if he could get his sister acquitted. William set off to find his sister's lover, the man she claimed killed his young nephews. After many days of searching, he found the man living and working on a farm in New Jersey.

When William confronted the cad, he denied ever having known of Elizabeth. Stonewalled, William returned to Philadelphia and began to collect a list of eye witnesses who had seen the man in Philadelphia and in the company of his sister.

The Christmas holidays were approaching and his time was running out. Adversely, he became ill from traveling in the harsh Pennsylvania winter, which can be almost as brutal as in New England. He became bedridden around Christmas and spent days recuperating at a friend's house in Philadelphia. Luck was not with him.

When he reached the Chester County jail, he was stunned to find that somehow he had lost touch of what day it was. He thought it was New Year's Day when it was actually January 2nd, just one day before Elizabeth's execution date, and he still hadn't gotten the evidence needed to save her to the council.

Riding quickly as he could, he went to the home of Ben Franklin, hoping to get Franklin to approve another postponement of Elizabeth's execution. Frustratingly, he had to wait several precious hours to see Franklin and when he did get an interview, Franklin felt that for some reason, it was improper for him to write the order for postponement of the execution.

Franklin sent William to a Charles Biddle, the vice president of the council. Now William was becoming frantic after spending another few hours when time was of the essence. William found Vice President Biddle at the statehouse in Philadelphia and convinced him to write the order: "Do not execute Wilson until you hear further from the council." Biddle knew the other members of the council were leaning towards acquitting Elizabeth and that they were probably going to revoke her sentence. William, the pardon firmly in hand, quickly started his twenty-four mile journey to Chester County jail, riding his horse straight down Market Street at breakneck speed. But Father Time was not yet finished with William as he rode to the Middle Ferry Crossing at the Schuylkill River.

The ferry was not in operating condition. Heavy rain from the previous few days had made the river rise to a dangerous level and the addition of large chunks of ice and other debris had made crossing it very dangerous at best, if not suicidal. The ferry was the only means of crossing the river in this area. A pontoon bridge from the Revolutionary War had washed out a few years earlier in another flood. Losing more precious hours after getting so close to saving his sister's life, William was not about to give up.

William pleaded and argued with the ferryman for hours, but the man refused to risk the trip across the ice-choked river. As his last resort, William drove his horse into the icy water in his own attempt to make it across the river. The horse did its best to struggle against the current and the subfreezing water and had managed to get William within fifty feet of the opposite shore. Then the horse was struck by a floating chunk of ice and sank into the watery depths.

Determined to reach the opposite shore William swam the rest of the way fighting the strong current and the effects of hypothermia. By the time he reached land, 3 1/2 miles downstream from where he first attempted to cross the raging river, he quickly found another horse and continued his life and death journey to Chester County jail. His route took him along what is known today as the Chester Pike.

Would luck hold out for Elizabeth Wilson? The Sheriff of Chester County, a man named William Gibbons, had hoped so. He was one of the many people who, after hearing Elizabeth's confession, was hoping she might be pardoned and believed that she was innocent. Unfortunately, the hour was fast approaching when he had to put aside his personal feelings and perform his duly-elected duty.

In order to help, he appointed men with flags along the Queens Highway. That way, if they saw William with a pardon, they could signal by waving flags and stop the execution. As the hour of execution approached, the sheriff anxiously awaited the signal, but as the hour struck twelve noon, the Sheriff could wait no longer.

Reluctantly, he gave the order and the cart supporting Elizabeth was pulled out from beneath her feet. By all accounts, she died without a struggle. But not right away. A few minutes after she was pronounced dead, the flags started waving on the road—too late to do them any good.

"A pardon! A pardon!" yelled William, as he burst into the clearing known as Hangman's Lot. At the site of Elizabeth's body hanging, his horse shied and reared up throwing William to the rain-soaked ground. Quickly taking action, Sheriff Gibbons cut the rope suspending Elizabeth and tried to revive her, but the deed was done.

Records vary as to the exact time that William actually arrived at the execution. Some claim he was twenty-three minutes too late; others state that he missed only by a few minutes. Regardless, of the time, when the crowd helped William out of the mud, another shock greeted them: William's hair had turned stark white and his once youthful face was marked by premature age lines. He started spouting unintelligible gibberish, entering into a state of delirium that was to last for several months.

So ended the life of a simple stonecutter, and began his legend as the Hermit of Pennsylvania. William eventually snapped out of his dementia and tried to return to a stone cutting life, but that was not to be.

From his harrowing ordeal, he lost all interest in being a member of society and eventually abandoned it all together. For seventeen long years, William traveled the wilderness between Chester County and Hummlestown, roughly following what would be known now as Route 322. Then in 1802, he found a cave system that would end up being his home for the next nineteen years. Gathering his few possessions, a straw mattress, a table and stool, some cooking utensils, a Bible, and a personal writing journal, he settled in to live a solitary existence, only interacting with the locals in Hummelstown, Campbelltown, and Middletown.

He made grind stones with which he traded for personal provisions with a local farmer. Even though his cave wasn't very isolated, William was adept at hiding in the caverns unseen. He kept his clothing clean, but stopped shaving and was always described by having a long white, flowing beard. He was a curiosity to the locals, and although they never felt threatened by his presence, it became a challenge to spot a glimpse of him. Sadly, after nineteen years of seclusion, on October 13, 1821, the *Harrisburg Intelligencer* ran this obituary notice:

> "Died at his lonely hovel among the hills, 12 miles southeast from Harrisburg Pennsylvania. William Wilson, who for many years endevoured to be a solitary recluse from the society of man... His retirement was principally occasioned of the melancholy manner of the death of his sister, by which is reason was, partially affected...(He) was observed frequently estranged, and one morning was found dead by a few of his neighbors, who had left him in the evening previously in good health."

Not long after his death, tales of Williams' spirit and that of his sister began to surface. It's been said that most hauntings occur because the ghost, or ghosts, have suffered a great trauma or because of unfinished business. Both of these factors play heavily in the history of William and Elizabeth Wilson.

William's spirit has been allegedly seen haunting his old cave, but as difficult as it was to spot him while he was alive, one can only believe that the only way to spot his ghost is if he really wants you to see him. Although, according to a former tour guide at the caverns, he claims that he used to have to go down into the caverns in the dark to open them up for the day's tours and has had several strange encounters, including hearing footsteps and the feeling he was being watched.

Strangely, Elizabeth's spirit has also been spotted near the cave. When the owner cut down trees in and around the cave to make a parking lot for the tourists to Indian Echo Caverns, the spirit of Elizabeth Wilson manifested. While alive, she had never been anywhere near the area. Perhaps she's seeking the spirit of William who haunts the cave?

In their home county of Chester, Bradford Township, there are tales of a female spirit, who is supposed to be a Elizabeth. According to some witnesses, her spirit searches through fallen leaves. Supposedly she's looking for the bodies of her murdered children. There's even a story about a phantom horseman who's been seen galloping across Delaware and Chester County and ends up at the old Chester County jail where Elizabeth was held prisoner before her execution. The problem with this tale is that it became well known after William became a hermit, but was repeated long before he actually died.

To get to the Indian Echo Caverns take Route 322 west, then take the Middletown/Hummlestown exit and follow the signs one half mile to the Caverns.

Emma is Here!
Haunts of Alfred's Victorian Restaurant

Tucked away, in the small town of Middletown, Pennsylvania, west of Hershey, there's a fine dining Italian restaurant known as Alfred's Victorian. It's a Central Pennsylvania landmark, widely known for its award-winning cuisine and is on the national register of historic places. Since 1970, Alfred Pellegrini and his family have owned the restaurant and have played host to its most famous resident spirit, Emma Young.

Built in 1888, by Charles Raymond, the mansion was constructed of brownstone from the nearby Hummelstown Brownstone Quarry. Charles Raymond, spared no expense in building the home. Joseph Dise of Spring Glen, Pennsylvania, was the architect.

Unfortunately, even in those days, people extended their credit too far sometimes; Raymond lost the property in foreclosure to the Middletown National Bank in 1896. Two years later, in 1898, the second owner, Radsicker Young purchased the mansion, for the price of $6,600.

Supposedly, the spirit of Radsicker is still hanging about the upstairs of the property. A psychic who visited the restaurant made contact with his spirit who told her: "Emma is here!" But evidently, Mr. Young likes his privacy. After the psychic started snapping some pictures, he bluntly told her to: "Get out."

Emma's playful spirit resides at Alfred's Victorian Restaurant.

In 1902, Radsicker sold the property to Simon Cameron Young. It's Simon Young's second wife, Emma, who is the most active spirit of the restaurant. Even though she died in 1948, she still likes to make her presence known.

According to Alfred's Victorian Web site, Emma and another female spirit named Eliza still dwell within the building. Some of the unexplained occurrences over the years have been attributed to Emma's ghost. A rocking chair that belonged to Emma has been seen rocking back and forth with no visible person sitting in it. Emma's trademark lavender perfume has been scented throughout the building and there have been times when both the restaurant staff and patrons have heard the disembodied sound of a woman's voice out of nowhere. Her spirit has been known to toss objects and rearrange furniture.

Emma, like many spirits, likes to fiddle with electronic objects from time to time. When Alfred purchased the Union Street mansion, it was with the intention of renovating it into a unique and elegant dining experience. So with all the improvements that he made, who wouldn't want to stay there? Emma sure does!

To get to Alfred's Victorian Restaurant from Hershey, take Route 322 west to the Middletown/Hummelstown exit, turn left onto Waltonville Road, then turn right onto US 322 west. Turn left onto Middletown Road. Middletown Road becomes Vine Street. Turn right onto East Main Street, and then turn left onto North Union Street. Alfred's Victorian will be on your right at 38 North Union Street.

Chapter 10
Hauntings North of Hershey

The Red Eyed Ghost

North of Hershey, there's the small isolated town of New Bloomfield—home to the Carson Long Military Institute. The modern descendant of the Bloomfield Academy, a Latin and grammar school, it was founded in 1836.

The spirit of a former commandant has been spotted outside The Maples.

Carson Long is the longest tenured military school in the United States. I'm sure many a young boy who misbehaved was threatened by their parents to be sent there for discipline, but the prospect of being sent away to a boarding school pales in comparison to tales of spirits and haunts throughout the academy.

The Carson Long Military Institute is a boarding school for boys grades six to twelve. Once, it accepted both male and female students, but now it only accepts male students. It's the oldest prep school in the United States that still requires military training for all of its students.

The school's campus is immense, spanning over 400 acres. There are two campuses, the main one is 57 acres in New Bloomfield, the other is Camp Carson, which consists of 350 acres along Sherman's Creek.

The ghost sightings have all occurred on the main campus. There are a total of nine buildings on the main campus. The Maples is the oldest. It dates back to 1840, and was the original living quarters and classroom for all the cadets. It also doubles as a reception hall and a museum, housing documents and school artifacts. Additionally, it serves as the residence of the president, Colonel Matthew J. Brown.

The previous president, Colonel Carson Holman, denied that there were any ghosts on campus and claimed that no student had ever died there. Other people have a different opinion. Some of them feel that The Maples is haunted.

It's been rumored you can see a pale figure looking out of the bay window. There's been speculation that it's the ghost of Carson Long, but if that's the case, then his spirit has traveled a long distance from where he died. Long, for whom the school was named, probably never even set foot in it. He was killed in a logging accident at a very young age in the Pacific Northwest. The name was given to the school by Theodore K. Long, Carson's father.

Theodore Long was a graduate of the Bloomfield Academy and also a graduate of Yale University. He purchased the school in 1914, and two years later renamed it the Carson Long Military Institute as a memorial to his son. So, it's more likely that the spirit is either Theodore Long, Carson's father, or the spirit of an old commandant of the school that is also known to walk the grounds outside The Maples.

Whoever the spirits are, they are very active. There have been reports over the years of disembodied voices, poltergeist activity involving doors opening and closing, and electrical equipment malfunctions (being turned on and off by themselves). Even museum exhibits and documents have been mysteriously moved from one spot to another.

There are four buildings that serve as classrooms and dormitories for the faculty and students: Centennial Hall, Willard Hall, Building #49, and Belfry Hall/Belfry Hall Annex. All of these buildings have spirit activity.

Reminiscent of the Canterville ghost's bloodstained hearth that can't be cleaned, there's a report that a mysterious pool of blood exists that cannot be cleaned, located on the outside of one of the dorms where a cadet who crashed a sled into the wall and died.

It's been reported that there was a fire in one of the buildings and you can still hear the screams and the crackle of burning fire coming from a boiler room where a commandant's wife perished in the flames.

One of the most famous ghosts of the school is the Phantom Drummer. Legend has it that a cadet drummer died of starvation after accidentally locking himself in one of the attics—he was never found. People claim that if you listen carefully, you'll be able to hear the faint drumming sound begin after *Taps* has been sounded for the night.

A more recent tale involves a cadet who died from a fatal fall. The student was, what they called, huffing aerosols. While he was high on the fumes, he fell down the stairs and died from his injuries (another good reason for not doing drugs). Now, people claim they hear the sound of him walking up and down the steps.

Many students over the years were probably sent there by their parents in order to discipline them after all other methods failed. So, this next haunt could very well have the basis of truth to it. After being disciplined, a cadet hung himself in his dorm room. Then,

Is the Holman Chapel haunted by a red-eyed ghost?

What's the mystery behind the eagle carving that unearthly glows red from time to time?

once the cadet was dead, other cadets reported seeing flickering lights and strange unexplained shadowy figures in the room.

Another haunted building is The Edward L. Holman Memorial Chapel. It's haunted most appropriately, by the man it memorializes, Colonel Edward L. Holman.

Colonel Holman had the distinction of serving the longest term as president. He served from right after World War One until his son, Colonel Carson R. Coleman, took over the presidency in 1971. In 1919, senior Colonel Holman was credited with introducing a National Defense Cadet Training program.

Colonel Edward Holman's red-eyed spirit is reputed to haunt the chapel that bears his name. His portrait is hanging in the chapel and it is said to follow you with glowing red eyes around the church. Also, for some reason, a sculpted eagle carved above the chapel doors will glow with a red unearthly luminescent light.

Colonel Matthew J. Brown is the current president—the first one since 1918 who is not descended from the school's founder. The year 2008 marks the 172nd year of the character building education at the Carson Long Military Institute and also 172 years of haunted history.

To get to The Carson Long Military Institute, take Route 422 west to 322 west, merge onto I-83 north, and then merge onto I-81 south exit 51A. Merge onto US/Route 11/15 north and take exit 65 towards Marysville. Take PA 274 to Duncannon/New Bloomfield, turn slight right onto South Main Street. Go straight to North Carlisle Street. The Carson Long Military Institute will be on your left.

The Haunted Amity Hall Hotel

There is an old hotel, that's been abandoned for at least twenty-five years outside of the town of Duncannon, north of Hershey, Pennsylvania. The town called it Amity Hall (not to be confused with Amityville, New York—that's a whole other paranormal ball of wax).

The Amity Hall Hotel has a history reaching back to the 1800s when it was built. During the years when the Pennsylvania Canal system was in use, travelers along the canal route would frequently lodge there. During the Civil War, it was used as a hospital. Perhaps some of the hauntings stem from this, although the most famous haunting has a more recent and tragic history attached to it, involving a gruesome multiple murder and suicide.

According to unofficial reports, a man and his wife and two young children were staying at the hotel; he left to conduct some business. In the meantime, while he was gone, his unfaithful wife met her lover there, and while in the throes of passion, her husband returned unexpectedly and found them together. In the heat of the moment, he promptly pulled out a revolver and shot his wife, her lover, and his two small children. Summoned by the sound of gunshots, the hotel security became involved in a running gun battle with a deranged husband resulting in one guard's death before the man was gunned down by the local law enforcement as he ran across the lobby. That's one version of the story.

The other version is similar, except that the man went mad for no apparent reason, and either stabbed the wife and killed her, or beat and the children to death. Sources differ about where the murders took place in the hotel as well. Some claim the man stabbed his wife in the upstairs attic. While other reports place the scene of the crime as a beating that took place on the front porch of the hotel. The children were either killed in the attic or on the second floor.

Regardless, the Amity Hall Hotel has been abandoned and closed for a good number of years and has fallen into a dismal state of disrepair. Over the years, many different paranormal events have been reported at the old hotel.

Those who have gone there have reported strange lights and faces peering out of the broken windows. The spirit of the wife who was murdered by the madman tends to manifest on the second floor of the hotel as either a full-bodied apparition at the top of the stairs or as a light floating along the moldy hallways. She's also been spotted floating through the nearby woods.

A word of caution to any male who intends to visit the hotel. She's said to be a malevolent towards men, and if the story surrounding her death is true, she has every right to be a bit vengeful. She makes her presence known to them as an intense cold spot or they tend to feel oppressed in her presence. She has also been known to slam doors in their faces.

According to some investigators, the worst manifestations occur in the trophy room upstairs. People who have investigated this room claim that, almost unanimously, they have all felt that whatever haunts that room violently wants them to leave.

People have reported seeing a very faint white figure of a woman in an attic window facing the parking lot. Also, white flashes of light have been spotted from those same windows. Even though the building has been boarded up for years, the board's keep coming off the second floor windows as if they were broken off and thrown.

More often than not, people who have gone there to look and take pictures claimed the batteries in their cameras quickly drain power. One seeker of the paranormal claims that spirits aren't limited to the inside of the Amity Hall Hotel. The claim is that small points of bluish light flooding around the corner outside the L-shaped building have been seen, and that black shadow-like figures about the size of a dog, but not dog shaped, linger out round the parking lot.

Whatever presence is there, it likes to drain the batteries from cell phones, too. One intrepid, if inexperienced, group of paranormal investigators, related this tale of their adventure to the Amity Hall Hotel.

One night, when they arrived at the decaying old hotel, they turned off their car and waited outside in the dark, lonely parking lot. Since many of the paranormal encounters happen outside of the hotel, they felt they had a good chance of seeing something. Besides, the hotel is private property and is heavily posted with no trespassing signs and the police cruise the area on a regular basis. The leader of the group, crawled out onto the sunroof of his car and attempted to take some pictures of the building hoping to catch something on film. Suddenly, for no apparent reason, his digital camera shut off. He only managed to snap four pictures before the batteries died. They were new and fresh batteries. He checked his cell phone. The batteries were also dead, and not surprising, so was everyone else's is in the group.

As a group, they decided to explore the outside of the hotel, technically as long as they didn't enter the building, they felt they were not trespassing. Shutting off the car headlights, they noticed strange shadows moving around the hotel, but no faces or lights in any windows of the inside of the decrepit building.

After forty-five minutes of exploring they decided to head for home. As they headed towards the main road, one of the group shouted that he'd seen the shape of a woman in the woods reflected off the car's headlights as they drove by. Quickly sensing that whatever forces in the vicinity were not friendly, they floored the gas pedal and sped home, convinced that the Amity Hall Hotel might truly be haunted after all.

The Perry County Historical Society do not record that any murder took place at the hotel at any time in its history. Sometimes legends are just that, legends. But you never know, because usually, behind every legend, there's a kernel of truth.

No directions will be provided as this is a private property with *No Trespassing* signs clearly marked.

The Ghosts of the Greenhouse Mansion

The town of Newport, Pennsylvania, is just off Route 11/15 in Perry County and not your normal tourist destination. While not far from Hershey or Harrisburg, there's no real reason to go there unless you live there. Unless of course, you're interested in the paranormal.

One of the oldest and largest houses in town was the family home of the first mayor of Newport. It was a two-story mansion complete was some cement stone lion sculptures in the front yard and a full-sized carriage house with a gazebo in the spacious acre

The Greenhouse Mansion in Newport, Pennsylvania—home to several spirits. One of them is angry.

This is where the old man's face appeared in the top far left window.

that made up the backyard of the property. In its heyday, during the 1800s, it was probably the most fashionable and elegant residence in town and the mayor and his family must have hosted quite a few parties there. There were always rumors, though, that the house had been built over an old Indian burial ground.

Many years after the mayor was long dead, the house became the residence of the Chisholm family, and that's how I ended up having an encounter with the unknown.

James Chisholm, was the last surviving family member to live in the house. His parents and siblings have all passed away and Jim kept their ashes, as they'd requested, on the large mantle in the "family room," as he called it. James Chisholm was a very big man, not just in the flesh, but in spirit as well. Jim inherited a large family fortune so he didn't need to work. He spent most of his time volunteering for charity and nonprofit organizations and was a member of the Civil Air Patrol and an officer of a group called The Society for Creative Anachronisms (or S.C.A). The S.C.A was a group dedicated to living history, in the form of reenactment of the middle ages.

This is how I first became friends with Jim Chisholm. Many times he opened his home to the group for their use, and believe me, the house could have easily been made into a large bed and breakfast had Jim wanted to do so.

During the 1980s, the group used the house quite a bit, not only just for meetings, but as a weekend retreat. Jim was always happy to have company. As welcoming as Jim was, the house itself was another story—a ghost story, as a matter of fact.

By the time I had met Jim, his house, as large and grand as it was, was starting to fall into disrepair. Jim was a great guy, but due to his health issues, he was unable to maintain the mansion by himself. But he never felt he needed to hire caretakers.

The room that felt the uneasiest to me, and everyone else that visited the house, was the upstairs library. I had only been in there once, and as much as I enjoy sitting and reading in a nice library room, this one gave me the chills. There seemed to be a cold that permeated the room even during the hottest days in August. Jim always joked that whatever was in the room was harmless, but he admitted that he didn't like going in there by himself when he was alone in the house.

Another of Jim's friends, Marilyn, from a nonprofit group, and her husband, Bob, were invited to spend the winter at Jim's mansion, when their mobile home's heating water system was damaged during a bad winter storm. Marilyn was somewhat of a medium and said, she was always aware of a negative energy presence in the library room. Once, she said she was walking down the hall past the library and the door slammed violently shut just as she was walking past it. There was nobody else besides her in the house at the time.

Another house guest said that, one night, he woke up and went to go downstairs to get something from the kitchen. As he walked down the spiral staircase, he saw a faintly luminescent figure standing in the middle of the living room. According to him, it was very indistinct, but he got the impression that it was a Native American. He quickly changed his mind about going downstairs and went back upstairs to his room—although it took him some time to go back to sleep.

One of the last times I stayed in the house, I was sleeping in an upstairs bedroom across from the library, and in the middle of the night, I was rudely awakened by the sound of someone pounding loudly on the door. I ran to the door and opened it in a matter of seconds, but no one was there and there wasn't enough time for anybody to have hidden anywhere. I had a chilling feeling it was whatever lived in the library room making it's presence known once again.

In 1989, I moved to Williamsport, Pennsylvania, and hadn't seen or heard much from Jim. When I was engaged to be married to my first wife (who is now my ex), a few years later, I'd tried to contact Jim but could never get him on the phone, and although I knew how to get to his house, I wasn't sure enough of the address to mail him an invitation. So one Saturday, when my fiancé and I were in the area of Newport, I suggested delivering the wedding invitation in person, as it would also give her a chance to meet Jim.

The mansion looked the same as I'd remembered and maybe a little more in need of a good paint job. But it had always needed that since the first day I saw it. Jim's pickup truck was parked in his usual spot, so I figured he was home. I knocked on the small side door that was used as the main entrance.

Usually, when Jim was home, he didn't lock the doors. It was hard for him to hear when someone was knocking because the house was so big. I knocked again at the door and tried turning the knob, it turned, but the door wouldn't budge. I tried pushing on the door and then gave up. There was a second door that was usually open on the other side of the house, too, so leaving my fiancé at the main door, I ran around the side of the house. No good; that door was stuck, as well!

I came back to where my fiancé was waiting. She was looking up at one of the second-floor windows. I glanced up in time to see the curtain move. She said that someone looked out from the window and it was old man who glared at her and then closed the curtain just as I showed up.

She had never met Jim and wouldn't have known what he looked like. I asked her if the man had a beard and she said no. It couldn't have been Jim; he always had a beard. I tried the door once more concerned that some stranger was in the house, but the door wouldn't open. Frustrated, we left, but before leaving I stuck the invitation in his mailbox.

A few days later I got a call from Marilyn. (She was the woman who had lived with him one year over the winter.) She explained that Jim had been in the hospital very ill for several weeks and probably wouldn't be able to attend the wedding, but he would really like to see me again and meet my fiancé. She asked if we would be able to visit him in the hospital soon.

Of course, I agreed to visit him the next weekend, but I had to ask her: If Jim was in the hospital, who was the old man in the house? The woman was silent for a second and then said, "There shouldn't have been anyone in the house. Bob and I have been collecting his mail for him, but the house has been locked and vacant since Jim went into the hospital. I hate to tell you this, but

I think it's "you know, you know who" from the upstairs library. I've seen him too!"

Sadly, Jim passed away before we got to visit him in the hospital. I attended his funeral and six months later, the Greenhouse was auctioned off and so was everything in it. The current occupant of the property is the city tax collector's office. Let's hope the spirit of the old man in the library doesn't give them any problems.

This is a place of business. No directions will be provided.

The White Dogs and The Hanging Tree

Outside of Liverpool, in Perry County, lived a man by the name of Davey Knouse, and he lived back in the woods along an all-dirt road. Years ago, he was driving home one night and claimed he was surrounded by a pack of spectral white dogs that jumped onto the roof of his car and bounced off the hood as well. And then vanished into thin air.

Legend has it, that the best place to see the spectral dogs is by the cul-de-sac near the dump by Mr. Knouse's farm. By the way, he died long ago, but the dogs are still there. Hunters passing through the area claim to have seen the same pack of dogs during the full moon.

What is it with Pennsylvania and packs of ghost dogs? Maybe they are the same ones that hound poor Peter Grubb. (See the tale, "The Haunted Hunter" in Chapter Seven).

Another haunt of Liverpool, is the old hanging tree. In the 1800s, a man was hung for a crime he didn't commit. If you drive to the tree and hang around till midnight, you can hear the ghostly sounds of that fateful day—crowds of people cheering, the sounds of crying, and a man screaming.

If you're really lucky, or unlucky depending on your view of the paranormal, you might even hear a swinging sound like that of a body hanging in the tree or hear the thump of an unseen weight land on the roof of your car. There's also reports that car engines and headlights cease to work there.

West Perry High School's Ghostly Janitor

West Perry High School in Elliottsburg, Perry County, has according to urban legend, a ghostly janitor. While getting the school ready for the coming school year, he was cleaning a window and lost his balance, falling through it and dying.

The window was in classroom 118, and since that tragic day, people inside the room have heard the disembodied sounds of a window shattering, the squeak of a *squeegee* on glass (probably the window), and the unnerving sound of a man screaming. The spirit of the unfortunate janitor has been spotted inside room 118 and in the halls of the school.

West Perry High School is located on Sherman's Valley Road. To get there from Hershey, take Route 422 West to 322 west; merge onto I-83 South Exit 51A. Merge onto US/Route 11/15 North and take Exit 65 toward Maryville. Take PA 274 to Duncannon/New Bloomfield; turn onto West Main Street and then onto Sherman's Valley Road.

Chapter 11
Dauphin County Ghosts

Ghosts of the I.H.S. Nursing Home

It's no great stretch of the imagination to expect a hospital or a nursing home to be haunted, but the I.H.S. Nursing Home, just outside of Hershey has the singular distinction to have been built over an old Native American burial ground. Supposedly, the left hallway unit on the main floor of the complex is the most haunted. Both the staff and residents of the nursing home have reported items being tossed by unseen hands and the sound of disembodied voices echoing through the halls.

On one occasion, a nurse walked into a patient's room to check on them for the night. She was called for an emergency and had to leave; when she returned to the room, the patient she had been attending to asked her a strange question. He wanted to know what happened to the little Indian boy that had been following the nurse. Needless to say, the nurse had no idea who he was talking about.

In another room, the patients had a more sinister encounter with the paranormal presence in the facility. Noticing that her roommate was having trouble breathing, the other resident in the room rang the emergency call button to summon the nurses. When the nurses arrived, the resident who was choking was suddenly able to breath. When they questioned her, she claimed that a ghostly figure that she described to look like the "Grim Reaper" was trying to strangle her. The nurses, at first, dismissed it as dementia—that is until the next day when the woman was examined and had bruises on her neck in the shape of hand prints.

The Haunted Mall

Ever hear of a haunted mall? Like houses, the longer a building sits empty, the more likely it starts gaining a reputation for being haunted. Stores aren't immune to this effect either, it seems. The Harrisburg East Mall is still actively used, during business hours. But at night, when all the stores are closed, one particular abandoned storefront may have some customers of a ghostly kind.

Many times, a store will close up in a mall and another store will quickly take its place. Not so in the case of the J. C. Penny closure. It sat empty for years, and during that time, several paranormal incidences have occurred. The security guards at this mall seemed to have their hands full. Many of them reported that as they walked past the abandoned store, they caught a glimpse of someone staring at them from behind the glass in the darkened store.

Not surprising since according to a former employee of the Penny's store, someone committed suicide there and another person died of natural causes inside the same store. According to the security guards, there were many times when the alarms would go off for no reason or the lights that were tied into motion sensors would turn on when no one was around the property. Probably the most unnerving encounters the guards reported happened nearest the old Penny's store. They all claimed that hey had the feeling they were being watched and felt as if someone were closely following them—so close, they could feel their breath on their necks.

During the summer, two guards claimed that they both encountered icy, cold spots inside the Penny's store; the problem was the air conditioning system wasn't working at the time. Needless to say, they quickly finished their security rounds and left the area.

The Linglestown Vortex and the Ghost Children of Gravity Hill

To the west of Hershey is a strange spot called Gravity Hill. The story goes that, in the 1950s, a bus load of schoolchildren went over an embankment and died in the crash. Since then, if you stop your car and put it in neutral, the ghosts of the children will push the car backwards up the hill so that it won't suffer the same fate as they did.

I decided to go there and put this urban legend to the test. I'd heard other tales of similar spots across the country, such as the Oregon Vortex, and was intrigued by having one in Pennsylvania.

A short drive off Interstate 83, to exit 35 and then South on Wyndamere Road/Highway 177 put me at the fateful intersection of Pleasant View Road. I then turned onto Pleasant View and made a quick U-turn. Looking out for any other vehicles, I put my car in neutral and awaited the miracle to happen. To my surprise, my car actually did start rolling back up the hill! I hit the brake and started my car up again. I drove to the stop sign and put my car in neutral again. I had to experience that phenomenon again. Sure enough, the car started rolling backwards uphill.

If you're ever in the area, be sure to stop and experience it for yourself. As an extra treat, take some baby powder and sprinkle it on your front bumper. It's said that the hand prints of the children will appear in the powder after the pushing your car uphill.

The Ghosts of Stony Valley

According to "spook hike" guide, Brandy Watts, as reported in the *Bushwhacker Bulletin*, in December of 2005, the old railroad bed that runs through Stony Valley Dauphin County has its share of ghosts.

Not just any specters; these haunts have a goal in mind. They're looking for their heads. The Stony Valley Railroad Grade trail is a twenty-two-mile-long, crushed stone trail that is extremely remote. While bikers and hikers frequent it to admire the view of the mounds of stones along the valley, one of the spectral hikers has a more focused reason. His name is Mason English and he was a young lad who made a rather bad choice in judgment. He was having no luck in fishing, so he decided to take a nap. He could have chosen a more comfortable resting spot and a less dangerous one, but he chose to take a nap on the railroad tracks of the Dauphin and Susquehanna railroad that ran through Stony Valley to Rausch Gap. It was a hot muggy day and the mosquitoes were terrible. The creosote covering the rails acts as a natural bug repellent, and Mason wanted some relief from their bites as he slept. He sought further protection from the bugs by covering himself with hemlock branches.

The engineer of the train only saw a pile of branches lying on the track as he ran over poor Mason English, decapitating him in the process.

English has been seen hiking the old line between Yellow Spring and Rattling Run. Evidently, like Joseph Baldwin, the ghost of the Macon County railroad line, old Mason is searching for his lost head.

Another ghost, who remains nameless, also haunts Stony Valley and has been seen in the area of the Kalmia Switch back. At least this poor spirit has a head up on Mason...He knows exactly where his head is, and it's not on his shoulders. It's in a wheelbarrow that he's been seen pushing around the Kalmia Switch back.

If you'd like to visit the Stony Valley Trail you might have to hurry. The National Guard at Fort Indiantown Gap has acquired the land and are considering using it as a multipurpose training range. One can only guess that the spirit of Mason English can't be too happy about being used for target practice.

Take I-81 to the exit for Lickdale/Lebanon Route 72, turn left onto Fisher Avenue, then turn left onto Route 72 north, pass through the Swatara State Park; the road will become Route 443. Take Goldmine Road to the top of Second Mountain and then descend to Stony Valley.

The Wolf Pond Monster

While this is a book about ghosts of Hershey and vicinity, I would be neglecting my duty as a collector of odd stories by not including this one. Located in Dauphin County, Wolf Pond is reported to be the home of an enormous thirty-foot reptile that's been described as a pike on steroids.

The creature is described as having black scales with yellow bands and a dark green scaly head measured at least six inches wide.

The fearsome creature was last spotted a century ago. But like its contemporaries, Nessie, the Loch Ness Monster and Chelsie the Chesapeake Bay Monster, you never know when it will rear its ugly head.

Charles Skinner, in his book, *Buried Treasures and Storied Waters, Cliffs, and Mountains*, reported that a fisherman was attacked by the creature and he hit it with his oar. In retaliation, the pond monster capsized his boat and dove back into the murky depths of the pond.

The Seven Elizabeths cemetery

You don't have to travel to Salem, Massachusetts, to encounter the ghostly spirits of seven witches. Not only that, they're witches with the unlikely coincidence of being buried in the same small graveyard in Middletown, and also having the same name— Elizabeth. The small cemetery is just outside of Hershey, on the way to Harrisburg.

All of the women were said to be witches. It seems strange though; usually they don't allow a convicted witch to be buried in graveyards with other locals. Supposedly, their restless spirits haunt the graveyard.

Legend has it that if you walk around the brick wall of the cemetery three times, you'll be pushed by these spirits.

Chapter 12

A Word About Ghost Hunting

First let me make a bold statement. There is not, and probably never will be, a right or wrong way to go Ghost Hunting! You're probably thinking: What? What about all those shows on the TV. That call themselves professional Ghost Hunters with all their fancy EMF Meters, digital recorders, and really cool black vans. Well, all that stuff is great, and truthfully, I'm a really big fan of those types of shows, but getting back to the point: As cool as those shows are, they don't hold a patent on Ghost hunting. That being said, I want to clarify that although there's no right or wrong way to conduct a Ghost Hunting investigation, there is definitely a right or wrong attitude to have when conducting an investigation.

I've been a member of several ghost hunting groups and they all have had different methods of investigating a haunting. Some were very oriented on the technical side of investigating. They liked to carry digital cameras, thermal scanner, and sometimes night vision goggles. To tell you the truth I wasn't sure I was with a group of ghost hunters as much as I was accompanying a squad of ghost busters!

Another group of paranormal investigators took a very different approach. They relied more on personal feelings and psychic impressions.

Both types of groups have their advantages and disadvantages.

Having been on many official paranormal investigations and a dozen walking ghost tours all over the country, my personal feeling is that ghosts were people, too. Some of the groups had a very official attitude and others were untrained, but enthusiastic about the possibility of seeing a ghost.

When I was a member of the Pennsylvania Ghost Hunters Society, we had strict rules we followed in order to keep everyone safe and also keep the data that we collected on the investigation as pure as possible for later inspection.

Everyone has their own instincts and talents they bring to a team of paranormal investigators and if you can figure out where your place on a team is, it'll make for a better investigation. For the purpose of this book, I put aside my professional ghost hunting criteria, because I just wanted to collect ghost stories and legends. It's not meant to be a serious discussion of the paranormal, but a collection of hopefully entertaining stories and a somewhat informative overview of the Hershey, Pennsylvania area and some of the surrounding counties.

Tips for the Hunter in All of Us

Even though this isn't a book on ghost hunting, and rather a collection of spooky stories, being a ghost hunter—or as I like to call myself a ghost watcher—I wanted to add some tips and personal anecdotes to help make your own ghost investigates more enjoyable.

One of the first questions people ask me is: Where do you find out about places that are haunted? When I first started ghost hunting twenty years ago, it was a lot harder than it is nowadays to find haunted locations. Back then, the only books available were books by Hans Holzer, Charles Berlitz, and other big name paranormal investigators—and they hardly ever wrote anything about the area I lived in. And they certainly didn't write about small-town local haunted places. But things have changed.

One of the best places to go for information is your hometown local historical society. If they don't have any written information, it's more than likely that they will know someone who works or volunteers there who will be able to point you in the right direction to somebody who has heard of a haunted location.

One of the first investigations that I ever participated in came as a tip from the Lancaster County Historical Society. I was in high school and wanted to do a paper on local hauntings. After talking to a person at the Historical Society I was pointed to a house on the south side of Lancaster County on Buchmiller Drive. It was a very good lead and resulted in my getting an excellent paper written, plus while I was there, I managed to get some good Electronic Voice Phenomenon (EVP) captured on tape.

Another place to look for haunted sites, now that we're in the age of the Internet, is online. Many Web sites are now devoted to ghost hunting and haunted locations. There's never been more information available for the budding ghost hunter. In fact, many of the ghost hunting groups share information with each other on line and off. Most of the haunted Web sites will have pictures taken from their investigations and will usually have a set of directions on how to get to a location if appropriate.

Once you've found a location to investigate, the real work is ready to begin. You and your ghost hunting group are going have to do some research. If the location you're investigating is a public one, you might want to just take a casual tour of the site to make sure that it's worth your while. Most places that give tours to the public will be happy to answer any of your paranormal-related questions and I've found in the past that once you ask the question, there's usually a tour guide or two who will have at least one story of a personal paranormal experience. If they don't, they'll know someone who has.

When you first form a ghost hunting group, unless you have some very good contacts, you're probably not going to get free access to the building. If your group goes through the correct channels and contacts the owners of the building or property, you'll have a better chance at doing a full-scale nighttime investigation.

Whatever you do, if you remember nothing else of what I'm telling you, remember these two words: **DON'T TRESPASS!** No paranormal investigation is worth being fined hundreds of dollars and possibly spending a night in jail.

The same rules doubly apply for private property haunted locations. If you get a referral that someone owns a haunted property, go through the correct channels to seek an investigation. No one wants strangers showing up unexpectedly on their doorstep asking if they have ghosts.

When you go on a ghost investigation, you don't have to have all sorts of fancy equipment. But it helps. Really, all you need is an open mind and either a notebook and a pen or a recording device to take verbal notes. Of course the more equipment you do have, the more various types of data you can collect.

One of the best tools you have at your disposal doesn't even cost any thing. It's called common sense. If you know you're going to be working in a dark, unfamiliar environment (and most times, that's the least of what your situation will be), always have adequate light sources and don't wander off by yourself. That's just plain common sense—and it doesn't cost a cent.

Whenever my old ghost hunting group would do an investigation, we would always be in teams of two or three members for both safety reasons and to have a witness should you run into paranormal activity.

Now let's talk about some of the equipment you might want to consider taking on a paranormal investigation. I'm not talking about the fancy hi tech stuff you see on television; I'm just talking basic equipment. One thing you'll probably want to have is a good camera. It doesn't have to be any kind of fancy digital one; it can just as easily be a cheap 35mm film camera.

The emphasis these days seems to be on digital cameras, but as a certified photo-specialist I can say this: If you can capture an image on regular film that looks even close to being an apparition, you'll be more convincing to skeptics. (If you care...) Why? Simply because it's very difficult to doctor a film negative and get away with it. A lot of times people will dismiss a digital image as being faked, where it's very difficult to fool an expert film developer. So, again, if you want to spend hundreds of dollars on a fancy-schmancy digital camera that's fine, be my guest. Just be aware that you really don't have to, to get a ghost picture.

Go through your old family photo album. Many times you'll find that you might already have a ghost picture. Some of the best paranormal photos I have, I've gotten from developing family gathering photos and on vacations. So don't underestimate photo evidence you may already have in your possession. As Gil Grissom says on *CSI*, " Always follow the evidence. Because the evidence doesn't lie."

Another inexpensive but valuable piece of equipment is a recording device. Here again, you don't have to spend a lot of money to get a piece of equipment you need. Sure, a digital recorder is nice, but a mini cassette recorder will work just fine for a fraction of the cost.

I'm sure you've seen the a fancy piece of equipment that some ghost hunting groups like to use called an Electromagnetic Field Detector (EMF). Did you know that you don't have to order one online and can usually get it at any hardware store for less than ten dollars? I picked one up years ago at my local department store for $ 9.99 and the other members of my group had spent much more than that on theirs—and mine worked just fine.

A thermal scanner is another fancy name for a thermometer. You'll see ghost hunters carrying what looks like a small pistol that has a laser sight and a digital led screen; they're nice to have, but here again, just go to your local hardware store and pick up a small portable digital thermometer for a few dollars. It doesn't have to be fancy; it just has to read temperature changes.

That covers the basic equipment that a paranormal investigator needs to do a quality investigation. A protective case would be helpful to transport you equipment, but you don't need to spend a lot of money on this either. I always used an inexpensive camcorder bag with lots of pockets and I've never had any problems.

Appendix

The Pennsylvania Hex Files

Hershey, Pennsylvnaia, is located in a region of Pennsylvania that is loosely called "The Pennsylvania Dutch Country. The Pennsylvania Germans, including Milton Hershey, who comprise much of the area have some very...shall we say, unique... superstitions and traditions.

Milton Hershey was proud to celebrate his Dutch heritage which is why the entrance to Hersheypark is themed to look like Rhineland.

Since this is a book about Hershey and the vicinity, a look at how the Pennsylvania Germans ward off ghosts and evil spirits would not be uncalled for. So, here's a brief look at some of the unique superstitions of the Hershey area starting with something everybody has seen but knows very little about: Hex Signs.

Hex Signs

Hex signs are both an art form and a tradition based on superstition. Every hex sign has a different meaning and some can be quite elaborately designed.

You'll find hex signs for sale in just about every gift shop in Lancaster, Lebanon, and Chester Counties; in fact, there's several stores that sell nothing *but* hex signs on various objects. You'll even find hex signs mounted on a few buildings in Hersheypark...for decoration, of course. As nice as they are to look at, hex signs perform a more serious function for some of the more traditional members of the Pennsylvania German community who use them as a symbols of protection.

According to German tradition, some hex signs will protect your livestock if placed on a barn, but it depends on what hex sign you use. Sometimes you'll see several different hex signs on one barn. They say that the signs will protect you from everything from pestilence to demonic possession.

The fear of witches and demons were a big concern back in the 1700s and 1800s, not just for the Dutch. We all know about Salem, Massachusetts, from history lessons in school.

The Pennsylvania Dutch felt that if they put certain hex signs on their houses and barns, they'd be protected from witches. But just what was a "witch" to them? When the Pennsylvania Dutch talk about witches, they're usually referring to a malevolent type of spirit rather than the green-faced, broomstick-riding hag that the term usually conjures up.

The best example from history is a famous entity know as the "Bell Witch." During the 1800s, a family in Tennessee was harassed by a spirit we would call a poltergeist today. It made noises, attacked members of the family, and even followed them to church and disrupted the service. But no one ever got a look at it, because it never appeared visually. Eventually, the "witch" went away, but not before killing John Bell, the family patriarch, with a vial of poison. This is the kind of entity that hex signs are supposed to protect you from. I'm sure once word spread about the Bell Witch, the signs literally flew off the shelves in sales.

PowWow

Hex signs weren't the only means of protection from the supernatural that the Pennsylvania Dutch had at their disposal. There's a whole form of folk healing art called "Powwowing" that they embraced as well. Powwowing was a more serious line of defense. It was widely accepted as an occult science and was practiced well up until the mid twentieth century. It's still practiced in some remote areas of Pennsylvania, but not as openly as it once was. There was at least one Powwow man or woman in every community.

Powwowers used a strong blend of Christian religious mysticism and pagan folklore, with a healthy dose of vaudeville stage magician showmanship thrown in for good measure to perform their cures.

With certain well-kept secret manuals passed down from one Powwower to another, they could supposedly cure everything from hair loss to casting out demons from someone who was possessed. Try getting that service from your HMO.

Witch Windows and Devil Doors

The Pennsylvania Germans were crafty, too. Besides hex signs and Powwowers, they would paint false doors and windows on their barns and houses. These fake thresholds were called Witch Windows and Devil Doors. It was believed that the evil entities trying to enter their homes would try to use these fake access points and crash into them, effectively keeping them out. They would keep them from coming back to plague them at a later date, as well.

Soul Hole

A lot of older farmhouses in the Pennsylvania Dutch country have what is known as a "soul hole" built into near the corners of their roofs. If devil doors and witch windows were used to keep evil spirits out, these soul holes did just the opposite. It allowed a spirit who was trapped in a building to leave and move on. In the days when most funerals were performed at home, having a soul hole for the recently departed made perfectly logical sense. Maybe the reason so many places are considered haunted these days is because they don't have any of these built-in soul holes. Try explaining that to your building contractors.

Bibliography

Books

D'Antonio, Michael, *Hershey: Milton S. Hershey's Extraordinary Life of Wealth, Empire and Utopian Dreams*, New York, NY, Simon & Schuster, 2006.

Jacques, Charles J., "Hersheypark: The Sweetness of Success," Jefferson, Ohio, *Amusement Park Journal*, 1997.

Whitenack, Pamela C., *Hersheypark/ Pamela Cassidy Whitenack*, Charleston, SC, Arcadia Pub., 2006.

Hinkle, Samuel F., "Hershey; Farsighted Confectioner, Famous Chocolate, Fine Community," New York, NY, Newcomen Society in North America, 1964.

Carmean, Edna J., "The Blue Eyed Six," Lebanon, PA, *Lebanon News Publishing Co.*, 1974.

Snavely, Joeseph R., "An Intimate Story of Milton S. Hershey," Hershey, PA, J. R. Snavely, 1957.

Shippen, Katherine B., *Milton S. Hershey/Katherine B. Shippen, Paul A. W. Wallice*, New York, NY, Random House, 1959.

Brenner, Joel G., *The Emperors of Chocolate: Inside the Secret World of Hershey and Mars*, New York, NY, Broadway Books, 2000.

Lake, Matt, *Weird Pennsylvania/Your Travel Guide to Pennsylvania's Local Legends and Best Kept Secrets*, New York, NY, Sterling Publishing Co. Inc., 2005.

Hauck, Dennis W., *Haunted Places: The National Directory*, New York, NY, Penguin Books, 1996.

Adams, Charles J., *Pennsylvania Dutch Country Ghosts Legends and Lore,* Reading, PA, 1994.

Guiley, Rosemary E., *The Encyclopedia of Ghosts and Spirits,* New York, NY, Facts on File Inc., 1992.

Tassin, Susan H., *Pennsylvania Ghost Towns: Uncovering the Hidden Past*, Mechanicsburg, PA, Stackpole Books, 2007.

Internet Sources

The Hershey Theater. www.hersheytheater.com

Shadowlands. www.shadowlands.net

Inn 422. www.inn422.com/history.html

Strange USA. www.strangeusa.com

Alfred's Victorian Restaurant. www.alfredsvictorian.com/history.html

Wikipedia, the free encyclopedia. www.wikipedia.org

Hershey, PA. www.hersheypartnership.com

Carson Long Military Institute. http://en.wikipedia.org/wiki/Carson_Long_Military_Institute

Cloverdale's Ghost. Braddock@hershey.pvt.k12.pa.us

Hershey History. www.hersheyhistory.org

www.ghostsofamerica.com.

Pennsylvania Haunts & History. http://hauntsandhistory.googlepages.com/pennsylvaniahauntsandhistory

Warshaw, Robin, Host to the ghosts, Online Periodical. www.robinwarshaw.com/clip3.html

http://www..liverpool.pa.net/stories/whitedogslegend.html

Places Index

Alfred's Victorian Restaurant, 124
Amity Hall, PA, 131
Amity Hall Hotel, 131, 132, 133, 134
Appalachian Trail, 109
Applebee's, 63
Apple Street, 77
Batdorf Building, The, 112, 113, 114
Belfrey Hall/Belfrey Hall Annex, 129
Buchmiller, Drive, 149
Boston, Mass., 60
Brandywine, Battle of, 60
Building # 49, 129
Campbelltown, PA, 122
Camp Carson, 128
Camp Silver Bell, 63
Carslisle, PA, 90
Carson Long Military Institute, 127, 128
Centennial Hall, 129
Chester County, PA, 118, 119, 121, 122, 123, 124, 153
Chester Pike, 121
Chicago, 12, 13
Chocolate World, 35, 45, 47
Cloverdale, 8, 49, 52, 53
Comet Rollercoaster, 32
Cornwall Furnace, 96, 105, 108
Crystal Lake, 116
Cuba, 56
Dauphin County, 103, 115
Derry-Church Township, 12
Derry Road, 37
Derry Township, 12, 13, 17, 50
Dickinson College, 90
Disney's Haunted Mansion, 62
Doge's Palace, 21

Duncannon, PA, 131
East Bradford Township,118
Edward L. Holman Memorial Chapel, 131
Elite Coach, 67
Elliottsburg, PA, 140
Ephrata, PA, 59, 60, 67, 78, 80, 86
Ephrata Cloisters, The, 59, 60
Ephrata High School, 62
Ephrata Hospital, 63
Ephrata REC Center, The, 73, 74, 75
Fort Indiantown Gap, 104, 144
Gettysburg, PA, 8, 84, 86
Gravity Hill, 143
Greenhouse Mansion, The, 134, 135, 139
Hampton Inn, 63, 64
Harrisburg, PA, 50, 123, 134, 145
Harrisburg East Mall, 142
Hershey Chocolate Factory, 15
Hershey Community Building, 19, 20, 40
Hershey Homestead, 50
Hershey Industrial School, 17, 50, 51, 55
Hershey Museum, 55
Hersheypark, 29, 30, 31, 37, 45, 56, 153
Hershey Stadium, 33
Hershey Theater, 19, 21, 22, 24, 26, 27, 57
Hershey, Town of, 7- 9, 15, 17, 20, 40, 45, 57, 78, 100, 105, 111, 115, 127, 131, 134, 141, 145, 148, 153
Hershey Trolley Company, 89
Hershey Trust Company, 50
Highpoint Mansion, 50
Honeybrook, PA, 69
Hotel Hershey, The, 20, 28, 35, 39, 40, 41, 44, 45, 47, 57, 58, 104

Hummlestown, PA, 122
I.H.S. Nursing Home, 141
Indian Echo Caverns, 115, 116, 117, 124
Indian Queen Tavern, 118
Indiantown Gap, 100
Indiantown Gap Creek, 102
Inn 422, 8, 89, 91, 96, 108
J.C. Penny, 142
Kalmia Switchback, 144
Kissing Tower, 37
Kleinfeltersville, PA, 110
Kleinfeltersville Hotel and Tavern, 110
Lancaster Caramel Company, 13
Lancaster City, 12, 13, 81, 84
Lancaster County, 50, 90, 118, 119, 149, 153
Lancaster County Historical Society, The, 149
Lebanon City, 96, 102
Lebanon County, 50, 90, 91, 100, 103, 105, 153
Lebanon County Historical Society, 110
Lebanon Valley College, 111
Lillydale, NY, 64
Linglestown Vortex, 143
Liverpool, PA, 139
London, 39
Mabel Silver Residence Hall, 111
Main Street, 62, 64
Maples, The, 127, 128, 129
Mary Capp Green Hall, 112
Maryland, 63
Memorial Field, 62
Mercersburg, PA, 90
Middle Ferry Crossing, 120
Middletown, PA, 122, 124, 145
Middletown National Bank, 124
Milton Hershey School, 8, 17
Moonshine Cemetery, 100, 102, 103
Moonshine Church, 100, 103, 104
Mountain Springs Hotel, 62
Mt. Zion Cemetery, 62
New Bloomfield, PA, 127, 128
New Ephrata, 67
New Jersey, 119
Newport, PA, 134, 137
Newtown Square, 118, 119
New York City, 12, 51, 63, 71
Northern Ireland, 90

Olde Annville Inn, The, 112, 113, 114
Old Lincoln Farmhouse, The, 67
Oregon Vortex, 143
Park Avenue, 37
Paris, 39
Pat's Hill, 40
Pennsylvania, 13, 115, 120, 124, 139
Pennsylvania Sons of America, 112
Perry County, 134, 139, 140
Perry County Historical Society, The, 134
Philadelphia, 12, 51, 60, 63, 91, 106, 107, 118, 120
Pine Grove Station, 109
Pleasant View Road, 143
Prospect Heights, 40
Rainbow Room, The, 115, 116
Rattling Run, 144
Rexmont Inn, 96, 97, 100, 105
Rexmont, PA, 96, 98
Rexmont Road, 96
Saint Anthony Wilderness Area, 109
Salem, Mass., 145, 154
Schuykill River, 120
Science Press, 69
Sherman's Creek, 128
Spooks, The, 64
Spring Creek, 30, 35
Spring Garden Street, 62
Stony Batter, PA, 90
Stony Valley Railroad Grade Trail, 143, 144
Strasburg, PA, 87
Super Dooper Looper, The, 34
Susan Amanda Room, 97
Swatara Creek, 115
The Loft, 38
Titanic, The, 55, 56, 57, 58
Washington State, 89, 92
West Bradford Township, 118
West Perry High School, 140
Willard Hall, 129
Williamsburg, VA, 60
Wilmington, DE, 71
World Columbian Exposition, 13
Wolf Pond, 145
Wyndamere Road, 143
Yale University, 128
Yellow Spring, 144